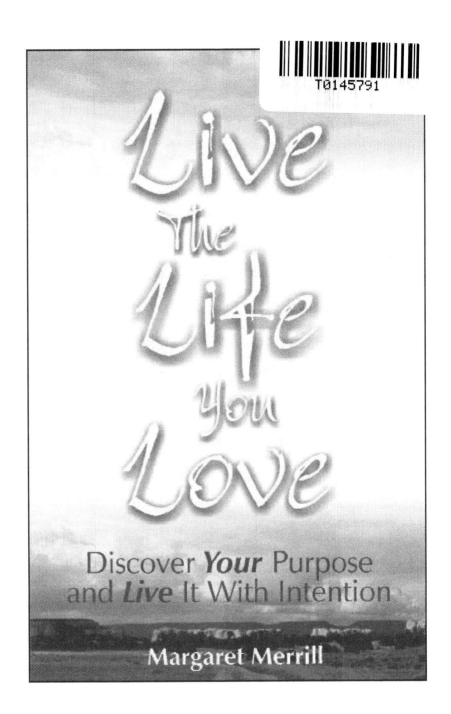

Live The Life You Love

Discover *Your* Purpose and *Live* It With Intention

Margaret Merrill

Morgan James Publishing • New York

Live The Life You Love™

Discover Your *Purpose* and *Live* It With Intention

Margaret Merrill

© 2007 New Vision Seminars Inc. All rights reserved.

Contact: Margaret Merrill
Voice: 888.214.7493
URL: http://www.fulfillyourpurpose.com
Email: margaret@fulfillyourpurpose.com

No part of this publication may be reproduced or transmitted in any form or by any means, mechanical or electronic, including photocopying and recording, or by any information storage and retrieval system, without permission in writing from New Vision Seminars Inc. (except by a reviewer, who may quote brief passages and /or show brief video clips in a review.)

ISBN: 1-60037-001-2 (Paperback)

Published by:

MORGAN · JAMES
THE ENTREPRENEURIAL PUBLISHER™
www.morganjamespublishing.com

Morgan James Publishing, LLC
1225 Franklin Ave., Ste. 325
Garden City, NY 11530-1693
Toll Free 800-485-4943
www.MorganJamesPublishing.com

Cover Design by:

G. Maurice Guinouard
3G Design Strategies
www.3g-design.com

Cover Photo by:

Wendy Hay
Hay Photography
www.wendyhay.com

Interior Design by:

Kimberly Lydon Stevenson
SpotCOLOR Design
kim@spotcolordesign.com

Limits of Liability/Disclaimer of Warranty:

No responsibility is assumed by the authors/publishers for any injury/and or damage and/or loss sustained to persons or property as a matter of the use of this product's liability, negligence or otherwise, or from any use of operation of any products, methods, instructions or ideas contained in the material herein.

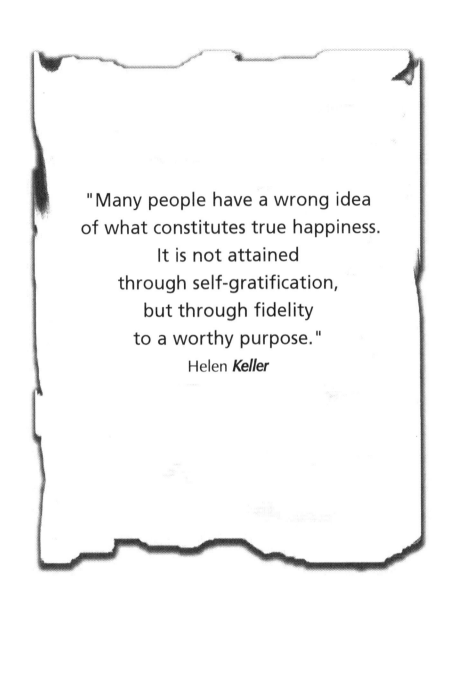

"Many people have a wrong idea
of what constitutes true happiness.
It is not attained
through self-gratification,
but through fidelity
to a worthy purpose."

Helen *Keller*

Claim Your
Free Bonus Here

A $97 Value!

Intentional *Goal Setting* Workbook to take you to the *Next Level*

How do you shift from
the traditional self-driven, goal setting process to
an *intentional* one that taps you into *infinite success*?

This *dynamic bonus* shows you how.
This gift is yours with the purchase of this book.
Download it *TODAY*,
so that from this day forward,
you cause *every goal* you set to be *a success*.

www.FulfillYourPurpose.com/bonus.htm

Dedication

This book is lovingly dedicated to my parents,
Bill and *Marie Koelbel*:
You both taught me that I could do anything that I desired
and that life's true meaning resides in service.
This book is evidence of both.

Also to my children, *Chris* and *Ryan*:
I love you both unconditionally
and am so very proud of the people that you are.

And to my friend, *Bob Proctor*:
Your belief in me has been priceless;
thank you for your contribution to the truth about us all.

Table of Contents

Live The Life You Love

VIII

Foreword

You are embarking on a powerful journey into meaning. Page by page, Margaret Merrill will lead you into the deep...provoking you to become totally honest with yourself. As she causes you to develop a new perception of purpose and intention in your life, you will become acutely aware that an individual who has never defined their life's purpose, nor understood living intentionally is living like a minnow in the shallows...awash by every wave around them, never expressing or adding deep meaning to their days.

Rather than merely reading this book, make a decision to complete each of the suggested exercises as they appear. Be aware that your old paradigm may tug at you mentally to just skip over the exercises and read on because that's what paradigms do. A paradigm's purpose is to keep you stuck where you are. The purpose of this book and the exercises it contains is to assist you in defeating your paradigms with every mental struggle you experience.

Finally, as you turn onto the last page, you'll have a smile on your face and a feeling of deep gratitude in your heart. You will feel as though you have left a dark room and are walking with a compelling new awareness into the bright clear light of day. Your life will be different, quite different. You will have a clearly defined purpose for living and will understand how to intentionally infuse your life with that mission.

Even though I have my purpose and values well established, which may be your case as well, reading each page has helped me focus on the important things in life. Before you read any further, I want to assure you that Margaret Merrill has not only done an excellent job in researching the information that lies within this book, but she has prepared this material based on personal experience. As I was reading the transcript prior to publication, Margaret's life reminded me of the Wright Brothers, when they were told they could not get their plane in the air and they answered, "I know I can, I just did."

Over the past few years I have watched her do everything she is suggesting you do and, at times, did it under a fairly adverse set of circumstances. However, regardless of how tough things appeared, this woman kept her attitude in check, kept a smile on her face and kept going. Margaret Merrill is an excellent author, businesswoman, seminar leader and mother. She has a talent for teaching challenging concepts in a succinct and easily understandable manner. She is living proof that the ideas you are about to study lead to the good life. Margaret has done a masterful job and I am fortunate to have her as my friend.

Bob **Proctor**
Chairman, Life Success Productions
"A Global Human Resource Organization"
http://www.bobproctor.com

"Our purpose is
the very essence of who you are.
It's what we want to be known for
and is a part of the
underlying motivation and driving force
which guides our actions
and brings us fulfillment.
Our purpose is bigger than we are.
Our purpose assists us
in making a difference in our jobs,
the lives of others, and the condition of
everything around us."

Bob *Proctor*

Chapter 1
Beginning at the *Beginning*

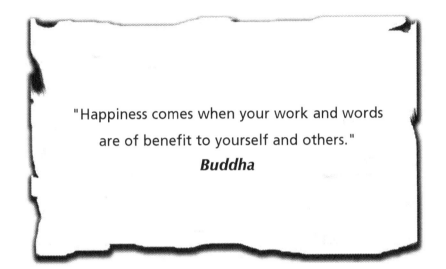

"Happiness comes when your work and words
are of benefit to yourself and others."
Buddha

It's calling...can you hear it? There's a restlessness that stirs inside you, waking you in the middle of the night saying, "I feel so unfulfilled. I used to be content to do what I do but not any more." You try to ignore it but it won't go away. You reason with yourself, saying, "You've accomplished so much already. You used to love this work. You really should be happy. Maybe you just need a change of scenery. A vacation might be good or some other big change...Yes! I could be a greeter at Wal-Mart." You muse on that idea for a bit. It sounds good at 2am.

You double your efforts at work and bury yourself in busyness but it surfaces again causing you to feel empty and to ask, "Is this all there is in life?" You know deep inside that it's time for a change but you wonder, to what? You ponder the meaning of it all. I mean all of it...life, love, work. Mostly you wonder about how to find the zest again that gave your life the juice that used to get you out of bed.

I understand. I was there, living in a place I loved but no longer wanted to live, at a job I had once enjoyed but had lost the drive for and in a relationship that was once a perfect fit but now left me depleted. I felt myself drying up inside, knowing I had talent crying to be expressed but seeing myself stuck, stuck and stuck. It was all the more difficult because I was also a personal development speaker. Somehow I felt I should have known better than to be in such a sad spot...Those cursed shoulds!

In those restless hours, in the middle of the night, I would think about the things I dreamed possible...way back when. What happened to the visions that used to fuel my life? Where was the joy? Yes, I found meaning in raising my children and in my relationships with friends and family but I had dreamed as a young woman of making a difference in the world. It had been my passion...Now I felt hopeless...even apathetic. Even though I had never experienced this, my inner knowing sounded the alarm. Like the buzz of a rattlesnake, apathy was dangerous and I knew it.

As I tossed and turned I didn't know that this past passion was stirring from its sleep and raising its voice to a roar. I finally came to understand that to save my own life I had to make a change. I had to grow.

My spirit threw a rope to my soul to save my life. That rope was the memory of my purpose. I always wanted to be an author and speaker, using my talents to help others live to their greater potential. Interestingly, the first person that my purpose was to save was myself, and save me it did.

It has guided my steps from there to here, from sadness to joy and from apathy to fulfillment. I am convinced that it is the most essential work any person must do.

That very cry for greater meaning is calling you also. It's what drew you here, in this moment, to this book. Your situation may be different but one thing I know for sure, we all crave meaning. We search for it. It's the very core of you calling to be expressed, not forgotten. Uncovering that core, helping you to recognize and reconnect to it's elements and then showing you how to bring that magnificence into your life and the lives of others is what these pages are about. I can speak with certainty about these things because one step at a time, by embracing growth, changing my thinking and with the support of God, mentors and my precious friends, I have done just that.

It's **time** for you to do the same,
to rid your life of discontent.

Life is far too short to live in "quiet desperation". It calls to you. You hear it. It wants to taste adventure, love deeply, give generously, create abundantly, and experience fully.

Completely magnificent and unlimited in nature, it is your essence. Through its' discovery you will experience true happiness, in its purest form. This is your mission.

As you unfold your magnificence, you will begin to experience its potent strength. It will give you energy beyond anything you have ever experienced. By living it, you will push past limitations and find reservoirs of courage and focus you never knew existed within you.

Growth is a part of our nature. We are either growing or dying. To grow, to give, to love, to belong, to be connected; all of these are the instinctive life force within us.

When we ignore this life force, it nudges us with discontent. If we don't listen, it calls with frustration. If we still refuse, it cries out with crisis, disease and depression.

Don Miguel Ruiz says that there are two ways to create our lives, we can either be the artist who creates life without awareness or we can rediscover our awareness and create lives full of adventure, verve and meaning. You are this second artist. You are here to rediscover your story and breathe it into your life through your purpose.

Our ***purpose*** is our personal mission statement.

I have had the honor of being a part of Bob Proctor's staff for over four years. He calls this discovering our worthy ideal. I have great respect for his wisdom and ability to help people apply spiritual success principles to their lives. Working with his clients I have seen that the purpose discovery process feels abstract and unattainable to most. It frustrates people because, like a child at the bakery counter, they can see the value of having defined a purpose, but they cannot navigate the barriers to savoring its sweet flavor. I do know that spiritually, mentally and emotionally, there is nothing more important or essential than this. Although in the beginning I felt embarrassed that, with all I knew about personal development, I was going through such life challenges. Now I see that it was perfect because I was aware of where I was and the growth principles I applied to get the results I have. My desire is to pass it all on to you and help you discover why you are here.

This may seem like a tall order especially when the idea of knowing "why" we are here can seem as slippery as a fish on a wet deck. Stop though, and think for a minute about a single isolated task, say... walking to a big tree and circling it for...how about 20 minutes. Why? No reason. Just do it. "You're crazy!" you say. "That would be a waste of my time!" "Exactly!" So, why would any of us go through our lives wasting our precious hours and minutes by not knowing why we're here, when we can be fully aware of who we are, what we value and how we can best use our talents and passions to serve humanity. With these few elements figured out, meaning and prosperity come tumbling in to your life like never before.

The clues to my purpose were throughout my life. I didn't have the tools to recognize them. It is these tools that I have assembled, through my work with Bob, my years on the Navajo Reservation and through personal research, that I share with you now.

I'll use my story as an example for your learning. I do understand that as we are all one spirit, my story is your story in many ways. The events that led me from New York to over twenty years of working with the Ramah Navajo people are fascinating and an interesting venue from which to teach. Be aware, as you read these stories, of what I valued and had most passion for. As I look back, there were so many clues. I was simply unaware. Now that I am aware I can use it as an amazing tool to help you.

The goal of this book is to use these beginning stories to raise your awareness of values and purpose from a practical perspective. Then I will take you through specific exercises to help you determine what you value most, what your talents and gifts are, to define your purpose and very importantly, to help you to use this information to create a powerful purpose-centered life.

I have always loved learning about different cultures. When I traveled to Italy during college to study the Renaissance, I lived with an Italian family, studied art at an Italian university and dated Italian men. When I did this...I just did it, without thought to why I did it. I only knew that I loved travel and that having an authentic experience with people of other cultures was interesting to me. I now know that this is a part of my purpose.

That passion for culture and adventure raised its head again a year later and drove me from my home and college in New York to a remote Navajo community in New Mexico. This school in this community fascinated me because the first Native group to go to Washington, DC and lobby for funds promised to them in treaties in the 1800's established it.

The power of purpose is passionate and driven to surmount obstacles that stand in its way. My trek across the Mississippi was small compared to the spirit that created this multi-million dollar project. History is shifted on the hinges of purpose. Here is a story of purpose that impacted Indian Education and sent it on a new, uncharted path. The courage of the people who traveled this path caused swells of self-determination to rise up across the continent, and then the world.

It began modestly. A group of community elders banded together and formed a school board. Their purpose was to build their own school. To do this they needed to bypass all federal agencies and contract directly with the government for funds to build this dream. It was a brave journey. What they were seeking had never been done before. Up until this point the Bureau of Indian Affairs handled education for these rural Native communities. This group of five set out for Washington, DC believing they could change that tide.

A Navajo matriarch, Bertha Lorenzo, dressed in a traditional velvet blouse, satin prairie-style skirt, turquoise and silver jewelry and a colorful wool Pendleton blanket was a member of the group that trekked day after day to their congressman's office. Their request was simple; they wanted a meeting to discuss their vision and the government's promise to provide teachers for native children. Currently their children were being taken two hours away to a Bureau of Indian Affairs boarding school. The parents were aware of the subtle and blatant abuses their children were suffering at the hands of people who were determined to wash them clean of their cultural differences.

Day after day they were brushed off in hopes that they'd lose heart and go back to the New Mexico hills. This congressional office had no idea of the heart and soul that these people embodied. Bertha, tired of the run around, arrived again at the congressman's office one morning and quietly spread her Pendleton blanket outside this very public figure's door. She sat down on it and stated that she would not leave until the money for her school was on the blanket. After a tense period of time during which I can only expect frantic phone calls were made, this wise congressman made a strategic decision and granted her wish. This victory did what every other triumph we experience does; it blazed the path for others to follow. With each of our personal wins, we create a clearer path, not only for ourselves, but for other.

Although road conditions and distances still require some to live in a dormitory, the distance in miles to the community school where culture is celebrated is very short.

The spirit of these people drew me. Although I couldn't name it, this project was one I wanted to be a part of. On a deep, spiritual level, purpose calls our souls to be a part of something big. When we take that first step, though, it can be down right scary.

As a lone student teacher with one semester of practical experience to go, I traveled to New Mexico thinking I was looking for adventure and loving the idea of learning from the Navajo culture. I found both and so much more. I was breath taken by the beauty of the vast vistas and huge sandstone monoliths that punctuated the rugged beauty of this land.

I arrived at the school having been dropped off by several student teachers who were heading for the "Big Reservation", suitcase in hand, ready to contribute. Rentals were scarce and my living budget was even more scant. I was offered a space in the dormitory and gladly accepted. It was far different from any other dorm I had lived in. It was a recycled army barracks.

The government beige cinderblock "isolation room" attached to the girls' dorm, reserved for ill children, became my home. I was excited. Coming from a family of six, this was the first bedroom with private bath that I had "all to myself". Although the experience was at times intensely lonely, as I dealt with the obvious differences between living in Albany, New York and what I fondly called the outback, I loved the land and the children's open acceptance. I had to finally limit visiting hours in my small room so that I could have a few moments to myself daily. During these quiet times the young girls would slip notes under my door on notebook paper with ragged edges, adorned with daisies and smiley faces, saying, "How are you? Me? I'm fine."

Those connections and the rich growth that ensues is the beauty of following that still, small voice that whispers of change. My memory is filled with the closeness I felt with these children. These times were a gift, given in exchange for answering the call to leave the comfort of my familiar life. Many such gifts continue to await us all.

I remember one beautiful child named Marion, who came from a traditional background and was very spiritually aware. We enjoyed walks together where she would explain the plants and their medicinal and cultural uses. In return, she asked if I would teach her Italian.

One day we dug up a Yucca plant and harvested the root, which she taught me to clean and crush the root with a rock. Then creating a milky, sudsy rinse by dunking it in water, she helped me to wash my hair explaining that this ritual was an important part of women's ceremonies. I was honored by her trust.

This same trust was extended to me many times throughout the next 24 years as I was invited to express my passion for teaching through my work with the Ramah Navajo community. As you will see, the journey with these people continues. Presently, their trust honors me again but in a new way.

Forever the student of self-growth, another of my top values, I read hundreds of personal development books while teaching at Ramah Navajo School to better my life and the lives of my students. This developed into a passion. That passion combined with my love for teaching took me to the podium in front of thousands of people attending seminars to better their lives.

The more I studied to better serve my students and audiences, the more I grew. The more I grew, the less I fit into my life. Truth was, although my values stayed the same, the venue for their expression had changed. I just hadn't come to terms with it yet. Like the hermit crab on the beach, I had outgrown my current shell and no amount of squeezing was going to make it fit. I was more vulnerable than I had ever been.

By being truthful with myself about my discontent I was able to also be truthful with those around me. I began the long journey of freeing myself to live the life I had dreamed of...a life I loved. It was during this journey that a Navajo medicine man named Howard told me I really was "Walks Far Woman."

A love for public speaking grew and then compelled me to train with Bob Proctor to facilitate his seminars. I taught during the week and built my seminar business evenings and weekends. After successfully facilitating over a dozen seminars, Bob asked me to join his staff. Working with Bob for four years has been the equivalent of a doctoral study in personal development. He is a master communicator on all facets of helping people globally to create their desired results through successful thought alignment. It is here that I learned about purpose, vision and goals.

As I took this understanding in to my work and conversations with others, I realized how little most of society knew about purpose as a foundation for creating success. I remember many conversations I had regarding life with a successful businesswoman who lived an abundant lifestyle. She obviously knew much about setting and achieving goals. Although an expert in her field, she felt empty and stuck. No matter how much she decorated, adorned and achieved, nothing filled the void. A frustrated hum interrupted her joy. She searched for the reason but couldn't name the cause.

Finally, I asked her if she thought that defining her life purpose would help. Being the "Type A" powerhouse that she was, she leaned back in her chair and replied, "We all want to know why we're here but how do we even begin to know what our purpose is? If you figure it out, let me know!" It was in that moment that I understood just how many people lived lives...successful lives that were without ties to true meaning.

The **truth** is, with guidance, people do figure out their purpose and you're about to be one of them.

All you need is guidance to uncover the answers that are already within you. The clues are everywhere in your life just as they were in mine. Think about the story I just told you. The clues were apparent in what I did for work and pleasure. They were evident in what I valued, my passions and what I lost track of time doing. I simply needed help clarifying what in my life pointed me towards my purpose. Once I'd found that, I discovered my internal compass. As any adventurer knows, once you find true north, you will never feel lost again. Through the shifts in venue and relationships that are bound to happen, you will always be solidly grounded in who you are at your very core. The work you choose to do will be meaningful and based on what you absolutely love to do. Imagine the bliss.

That would be enough for one day's work. However, living your purpose is as critical as defining it. Without the living application, newly revealed knowledge would get locked away in a journal somewhere and life would go on as usual. That would be a waste of both of our time.

Living your purpose will require change. When I look back on quitting my teaching job, going through a divorce, creating my ranch as a small retreat center and moving with my boys to the Scottsdale area, I felt like I took the puzzle of my life and threw all of the pieces into the air.

It was frightening at times. Knowing what I do about redirecting my attitude, I'd work to remind myself that there was no place I'd rather be than pursuing my dreams. There were times when I looked around my little house in Scottsdale and wondered what the heck I was trying to do. I just kept moving...no matter what. To this day I keep a quote by John Wayne on my refrigerator, "Courage is being scared to death but saddling up anyways."

That very act of saddling up allows not only ourselves but every project associated with us to grow also. My ranch in New Mexico is a poignant example of this. It was my home during my marriage and the years that followed as I continued to raise my children as a single mom. When we moved to Arizona it grew into a bed and breakfast and small retreat center. It is now reaching a new level of maturity. Sitting beside the Ramah Navajo community, I realized how this ranch, named Oso Vista, could serve both the Navajo community and the world. As I mentioned, I love authentic cultural experiences. Many people do. It is being launched as a cultural retreat and healing center.

Its name meaning bear view is derived from the north vista across a wide valley of meadows, Cedar and Pinion Pine trees to Oso Ridge. These mountains have many wild canyons that are home to bears.

The bear is also a powerful native totem meaning "The courage to speak your truth." This project with its cultural, spiritual and personal development aspects is my purpose, personified. It is this type of project, where you are allowed to speak your truth, that I desire to help you develop.

Our *purpose* compels us
to be better versions of ourselves.

It's our highest calling. There are many ways to experience this highest nature or calling.

For example, when I reached an at-risk student who was labeled "unreachable" or caused a young woman who was considering suicide to reconsider life, I was obviously living my highest calling. I experienced it in simple ways too. When I got Grandma Mary, an elderly Navajo matriarch selling green chili Spam burritos, hot coffee or "gohweeh" in Navajo in the morning...that was also living my highest calling. You and I do it every day. Why do these things feel so good to us?

Abraham Maslow talks about this in his fascinating work on self-actualization. He says that every person has an internal **need** to make the most of their abilities. A quote by Maslow that is often cited says that each person must be who they are at their very core whether it be a painter, writer or leader in order for them to be at peace with themselves and their lives.

If self-actualized people live **meaningful** and **successful** lives, how do we act more like them?

Maslow says that we must get real with our lives, allow ourselves to be freely spontaneous, be creative, solve problems, connect with others, enjoy life, live by our personal values and not judge others.

How does **self-actualization** relate to purpose?

When we have grown to the point that we're making the most of our abilities and serving others, we're living to our greatest potential. Dr. Wayne Dyer, in his book *The Power of Intention*, encourages people to remember that we are on purpose when we live for the highest good. Each act of kindness shown to any living thing fills us with the satisfaction that we are making a difference.

This is why we're compelled to **grow**.

This urge has been instilled in every cell of our body. On both conscious and sub-conscious levels we desire to grow. We take each breath in order to go on living. Our bodies convert food to give us the stamina for life. Our heart continues beating without a single conscious demand on our part. We are living organisms that crave fulfillment.

On the physical level we desire health and wellness. Intellectually, we seek knowledge and expertise. Emotionally we strive for understanding and connection with others.

Spiritually we yearn to know our Creator, experience creation and understand the oneness of all creation. When we experience our highest calling, we are experiencing all of these. Maslow called this "self-transcendence" and placed it at the top of the pyramid of self-actualization.

Living without purpose is like being the captain of a sailing vessel setting out to sea with unfamiliar cargo and an unknown destination. You become very busy sailing but not quite certain of the where and why of it. You travel port-to-port gathering trinkets and treasures, deciding your next stopping place based on the directions of passers-by. You sail and sail, too busy and distracted to go below the deck, shake the dust off the cover that lies over the cargo and take a good look. You hear a voice whisper quietly that the delivery of this precious cargo would give direction to the bow and bring untold joy to both the deliverers and the recipients. Yet, you do not listen.

Juxtapose that with this: You arrive at your sailing vessel, loving the magnificence of its carved mahogany and sleek lines. You heed a deeper prompting though, so you descend below the deck and discover the precious cargo that is within your ship's hold and realize your ship's true value. Sitting in front of this massive gleaming pile, it is clear to you that this cargo is priceless and must be delivered safely. You determine that it's your life's work to sail throughout the world delivering this cargo for all to enjoy. You notice that as you do this, the pile beneath your deck only grows. You understand, as you stand purposefully at the helm with the wind through your hair and the sun on your back, that the treasures you have left on the shore behind your wake have changed lives, causing your heart to swell with incredible joy and love.

As you watch the water before your bow, your realize that the unexpected benefit to you, the ship's captain, is that through the fascinating adventures of your travel you reach new heights of personal understanding. You have experienced a depth to your passions and talents that you didn't know was possible and have come to know the meaning of oneness with your creator. This feeling that you experience is enlightened self-awareness. You're so glad you listened to the call. And so am I.

"If we do not rise to the challenge of
our unique capacity to shape our lives,
to seek the kinds of growth that we
find individually fulfilling,
then we can have no security:
we will live in a world of sham,
in which our selves
are determined by the will of others,
in which we will be
constantly buffeted and increasingly
isolated by the changes round us."
Nena **O'Neil**

Live The Life You Love

Chapter 2

Purpose and *Life*

"A lot of people are waiting for Martin Luther King or Mahatma Gandhi to come back -- but they are gone. We are it. It is up to us. It is up to you."

Marian Wright **Edelman**

The biggest component of your purpose will be the service you will give through your talents, passions and gifts. Service is giving and has much to do with energy. All of life is about the flow of energy to and through us. Many people are gaining a greater awareness of this as quantum physics connects with spiritualism. Movies like, "What the Bleep" and "The Secret" are helping people understand these ideas. Each thought we think, each emotion we feel and each act we initiate moves the molecules of energy in the universe. This is why it's said that a stone thrown into a lake changes the shoreline forever. It is also why the work you are doing right now to create greater awareness is raising the collective energy of all mankind. Each act of kindness you do, each time you pick up a piece of trash or kindly allow a motorist to merge, you create an energetic effect on the world that moves everything into a healthier alignment.

An orientation to life based on service is the foundation to creating abundance. When we give for the sake of the love of giving, we open up our heart to receive also. This is called the cycle of giving and receiving. It is a natural law that operates in the world, just like the law of gravity. Raymond Holliwell author of "Working With the Law" says that giving is the beginning of all creation.

Let's talk about *giving*.
It's important to understand what motivates us to do it...

I have met many people who tell me that they give and give at their church but are wondering where all the riches are in their lives. They're waiting for God to "pay up". If we give to receive, as Bob Proctor says, "We're trading." If we give with the intention of receiving, our intention is selfish in nature and acts like a clamp that we tighten down on the flow into our lives. Giving to receive puts our minds into a state of "lack". We think that if we don't control the flow back to us by giving, then it won't arrive. When in reality, the flow desires to expand because abundance is the nature of the creative energy that we live and breathe in every day. Learning to truly give without thought of receiving is the best way to learn to trust that abundance. Each time you give think, "There's plenty to go around." That is why service is such an important element of our life purpose.

I've worked on trusting this abundance since I turned in my letter of resignation at the Navajo school I had taught at for 20 years. Although I understood that prosperity was only a thought away, there were times when I wrestled with lack and fear. The first thing I learned was to get out of the ring! Wrestling with lack would only keep my emotional ties there. I disciplined myself to focus on my purpose and the dream I had for my life and then I kept moving. The worst thing to do, would have been to do nothing.

I would hear Bob Proctor tell people to focus on **service** and the **abundance** would come.

Although it rang true to me, I didn't quite understand "why" but I chose to trust what he said until I did understand. After years of close association with Bob here is what I learned, service is the mental framework for creating the life you desire. Money cannot be the main focus. Wanting an abundant life is healthy and very much in alignment with your greatest good. If you want abundance but know that having money as your main focus is out of sync with your highest nature, what is your main focus? You get to that abundance through an unselfish focus on service and doing your very best with what you have at hand. As Mike Dooley says in his seminars, "Do all you can, with what you've got, from where you are."

In the years since I left the school I've completely focused on living the life I craved. That has caused me to get further out on a limb than I ever have been. Bob says that if you're not out on a limb you're just taking up space. I do know that embracing risk as an exciting part of the adventure has really helped keep my attitude on track. I remind myself frequently that there's no place I'd rather be than living the adventure of my life and that the Universe is friendly to my plan.

> Then one day I **made** the next biggest **shift** in my **thinking** and **realized** that I **AM living** my **dream**.

This was huge for me. Even if the evidence of my dream results were small, they were still there. This one realization accelerated my results exponentially because I no longer saw my dream as "out there". I saw it as "here and now". In the process of manifestation this shifted everything for me. I believed like never before because I focus on the small results around me, not their lack in my life. Look into your life. If you want to be an author, see all the times that you use writing to communicate your thoughts. That is evidence. If you want your business to grow, see the things you do well and focus on those successes. See the small ways you are already living your dream. In this way you'll act as the person you envision...because you are that person already. This will empower your visualizations like never before.

My love for the Navajo community that was my home for so many years has drawn me back. I'm working closely now with my dear friend Tom, who is a master communicator, with Howard, a Navajo medicine man and with many local and state Native leaders to create my ranch as a cultural retreat and healing center. It completely excites me to be able to offer the people of the world an opportunity to authentically experience Navajo culture and spiritualism and the people of the Ramah Navajo community a venue for traditional Navajo behavioral health services. This exciting purposeful project challenges me to grow in ways I could never have imagined.

Not long ago I walked on the land near my home with my medicine man friend while he chose the location for a 500 square foot, eight-sided, traditional log dwelling, or Hogan. This structure will be the center of cultural and spiritual healing at Oso Vista Ranch.

I'll never forget the moment. The sun was setting bright gold on a misty wall of rain that moved in from the west. The medicine man walked east and west on the north side of the adobe hacienda that offers itself as a small retreat center. He stopped in a small clearing on the northeast side and stood quietly for a moment. I stood in reverence of his prayerfulness. He broke the silence, "Here...this feels right. We'll build it here." I had been told by the Navajo builder, "We build a Hogan from the center out. Stake the center and we'll measure from there." I stood with a metal stake and hammer in hand, "Are you in the center?" I asked. "Yes, this is the center. We'll put the stake here." At that moment I was having the most amazing authentic cultural experience. I had never considered the building of a structure beginning with the center...but this was metaphorically and physically perfect. Was I living the dream of creating a cultural and spiritual center on my land? The evidence was so profound that it took my breath away.

The pursuit of your dream gives countless occasions to live it. It's important that we realize and not miss the joy of these moments.

I think the most beautiful thing about this project is how it serves. In very important ways it serves the local native and global community. Through this service it will prosper. Giving draws us to understand that we are all one, and that as such serving another in any way is serving the whole. This concept is one that Navajo people understand in a very profound way.

No act is too small. Helping an elderly person carry a bag of groceries, holding the door for the person behind you, giving a heartfelt compliment or listening to a grieving friend: all of these move our hearts, minds and souls to greater levels of awareness and give our lives joy and meaning.

Simply know in your heart that "Energy always returns to its point of origination." You will always be taken care of because the Universe is a friendly place. It may come from completely unexpected sources. Sometimes we make a deposit at the north branch of our bank and make a withdrawal at the south branch but the money is there just the same. Trust that as you move toward greater self-awareness you will be given every help you need.

I have no idea how to build a Hogan. I only have the vision. As Howard and I speak to people about what is needed, the resources and talent arrives. Our first investor has appeared. A kindred soul named Tom has provided the building capital. Almost immediately, a Hogan-builder with a crew of skilled Navajo craftsmen was provided, helping us determine how to hold to tradition as well as build a structure that will last.

We've needed logs. It's fall and already has begun to freeze. The Forest Service cut the logs we need last spring and interestingly Zuni Pueblo Forest Products still has access to them. Clifford, a Zuni Indian, who runs the operation, told me they're honored to be a part of such an important project and will hold the woodcutters back while his crew hauls from the mountains what we need for the project.

This is such a good example for you to think about while you build abundance in your job or business. As you desire to increase profits, think about where you will focus. You can focus on either giving or receiving. Increase your service and you will find your profits increase and people rush to support you. They sense the altruistic nature of your project. Their innate desire to make a difference and help another compels them to help you. Isn't it interesting to begin to see that the principles we live by personally are the same for business. We are taken care of when we take care of others.

This is just one more example of the beautiful way in which life satisfies our needs through our connection with others. Were we able to satisfy all of our emotional, spiritual and physical needs outside of relationships, the world would be a far less friendly place and we'd miss the richness of working with others.

I'm so grateful for the experiences that serving others is providing me. As we sat in my New Mexico living room, Howard explained how we needed the center of the floor to be dirt for ceremonies. He explained that sometimes the medicine man creates a sand painting with colored sand, on which a person sits during their ceremony. When the ceremony is finished, the earth is swept up and the sand and dirt is given to the person to spread around their home. I imagine many such ceremonies and the healing they will provide. Had I not ventured out on this limb, I would have never tasted such sweet fruit.

Eastern masters say that service is the path to enlightenment because it leads us into partnership with our Creator and a greater understanding of the oneness of humankind.

Before we think that service will lead us to living the life of a monk, I want to make the point that living our purpose is also fun. I can hear you breathing a sigh of relief from here. Yes, our purpose is to live our highest calling and serve but it's also to live each moment completely enjoying the beauty and love that is around us. Many call this living in the moment. The smell of rain on the pine trees, a baby's breath on our cheek, the scarlet of a sunset, a lover's kiss, a Navajo corn meal blessing, chocolate on strawberries...these are all a part of our purpose. They are our opportunities to receive from abundance. Let it in. Let it all in.

We are here to live rich, abundant, juicy lives, full of moments that fill our senses, hearts and souls with the enlivenment of connection with others and the natural world. Therefore, when my friend, Deborah, tells me that her purpose on this planet is to make and enjoy a peach pie from the fruit tree in her yard, she is entirely correct.

Life is to be taken in, drunk deeply, savored and enjoyed as we go about our journey of self-discovery and purposeful living. This self-discovery unfolds through our talents, service, joy and very importantly our relationships with those that our purpose benefits.

Connectedness is essential for healthy human growth.

I remember one particular Ramah Navajo health, wellness and education fair. The parents and grandparents of the community had driven out of the hills in their pickup trucks to see their children's art displays and learn more about raising healthy individuals. They were well aware of the problems on the reservation and many desired change.

I always love the juxtaposition of western and Native culture at these events. The school gymnasium with shiny wooden floor and sunlight streaming through high windows sported a team of a different sort that day. The uniform of cowboy hats, wranglers and boots was punctuated with the feminine energy of velvet blouses, cotton prairie skirts and silver jewelry.

I was milling around looking at the displays with men and women from the area. Suddenly, I was stopped in my tracks by a single display. There in front of me was an infrared photograph of the brain activity of an abused child who had not experienced healthy family bonding. One could see the dim mental activity, evidenced by disconnected, small spots of faint light in the four lobes. Beside it was a photograph of the brain activity of a healthy child with loving family bonds. The four lobes of this healthy brain were bright and active with large connected pathways between them. I remember standing in awe of the visual evidence of the philosophic, emotional and physical connections between intelligence and bonding.

Connection and relationships are essential. We all know the value of having people in our lives that completely accept and love us. Whenever we are with them, we are home.

It is also through our connections with others that we discover who we are. Our relationships are a mirror that when held up, the wizard inside asks, "How do you respect differences and find similarities? How do you accept and give your love, talent, and support? Do you see others in their highest light? Do you see how we all are connected?" It is through our striving for purposeful living that we come to a true understanding of the principles of non-judgment, respect, support, love and co-creative partnership.

Connecting to others who believe in us is essential in our quest to live ***meaningful*** and ***purposeful*** lives.

Bob Proctor has been an important mentor in my life. Three years ago, when I temporarily set my ranch as a bed and breakfast, left it in the care of a manager, loaded my U-Haul truck and moved my boys and me from New Mexico to Arizona, he continually expressed his belief in my ability to create my dreams and make a bigger contribution to the world. He was a strong anchor because I knew his wisdom and international experience working with people had given him a heightened ability for vision and intuition. Knowing he was there and believed in me was all I needed.

This belief and perspective created an anchor outside of my present circumstances to the shore of a new destination I had only dreamed of. His belief was so important to me because not everyone believed. The word around the ranching community, near the reservation I had taught on, was that I'd never make it and be back within one year. It shook my confidence and caused me to ask the question that most of us ask before making a life-changing shift, "Am I crazy?" I remember emailing Bob one day and simply saying, "Are you there?" He answered back saying, "I'm here." I answered, "Okay, that was all I needed to know."

It wasn't long after I left that others who were unhappy also chose to move on. As we live our purpose, we inspire others to do the same. I've found that I need not say a word. All I must do is to grow and follow my dreams. That simple act sets an example that causes others to do the same. Here's a mind expanding idea, because we are connected on a fundamental level, our growth toward our purpose inspires growth in all of humanity.

The beauty is that as we devote ourselves to living our purpose we also maximize our ability to manifest abundance in our lives. It is through serving that we are served and through giving that we receive. This is as it should be.

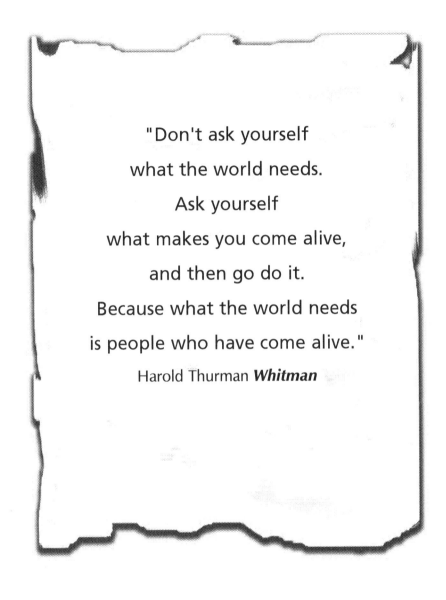

"Don't ask yourself
what the world needs.
Ask yourself
what makes you come alive,
and then go do it.
Because what the world needs
is people who have come alive."

Harold Thurman **Whitman**

Live The Life You Love

Chapter 3

What We *Value*

> "Never doubt that a small group of
> thoughtful, committed citizens
> can change the world;
> indeed, it's the only thing that ever has."
> Margaret **Mead**

Since our purpose is an outgrowth of our values we'll spend time here helping you determine yours. Many people have done values exercises as a part of business or personal development seminars. If you have, I encourage you to approach the idea of determining your values through this chapter with a fresh intention to learn more about yourself and apply this new knowledge to today's process of discovering your purpose. Remember also that each day brings you a greater awareness of yourself and what you truly value may be more apparent to you today than it ever has.

Our values are as individual as our voices and smiles. Some may assert that everyone's values are similar. For example doesn't everyone value honesty, faithfulness, and independence? Some may have these at the top of their list, some may not. I have no judgment on this as they are creating the experiences that they need in order to grow. As an example, if someone does not value faithfulness, then they will experience a lack of faithfulness in their life. That experience will cause them to have a greater understanding of the value of faithfulness. It's all in the learning.

Some may have the same values as another but will prioritize them differently according to the life experiences they have lived through. Losing a loved one can heighten our awareness of the value of friends and family. They often become precious as never before. In my case, the loss of my mother also caused me to look at time differently. Life was short; it was time to make a change. It was after her death that I chose to make big changes in my life. There are two ways to create change in our lives, emotional impact and repetition. This was an example of emotional impact.

Some experiences may cause us to rearrange our highest values. Some experiences may cause us to gain greater insight into others. This begs the question: If our values can change as we grow in awareness, are they good indicators for living and for the creation of a meaningful purpose statement? The answer is yes. As complex human beings, we continually flux and change. Embracing and allowing this flux encourages growth. The energy we spend in knowing ourselves better, even if it were just for this moment, is invaluable and leads us to greater self-awareness and depth of meaning.

Values are also sometimes culturally dependent.

For example, many Native people have a very high awareness of the value of sharing. They share support, burdens and belongings. When any financial burden befell one Navajo family, such as a funeral, wedding, trip, even college expenses, the entire extended family would get together and have a meeting. They would decide how the whole family could share the burden of the one. Sometimes the ideas generated would include having a raffle or putting a donation pickle jar, with a photo of the recipient taped to it, in the local trading post.

At Native social events, Pow Wows and traditional dances, I have witnessed many "giveaways". This is where the host family or community gives the invited guests baskets of food and gifts. It was fascinating to me to see women dressed traditionally handing out brightly colored plastic laundry baskets filled with fruit, bread, household and canned goods.

A feast at a Pueblo is also an example of this value in action. They are opening their doors to give to those who arrive. They understand that their life is lived in a place of balance between giving and receiving. They give for the joy of it and in reverence to the law.

When I went through my divorce I felt warm support from my Navajo community that gave me great comfort. My Navajo community, having lived through untold challenges, supported me with unconditional love and a complete lack of judgment. I'll never forget it. This may add greater meaning for you to the word "tribe".

The important thing here is for you to look at what you value without judgment or agenda. What another person values is simply their set of individual swirls and curls in the fingerprint of their personality. What you value is yours.

This is an excellent exercise to do with your partner. Learning what another values and then paying special consideration to those values is an act of respect that builds trust.

I remember an early experience I had when this understanding of individual perspective was just budding in my mind. I read the book *The Five Love Languages* by Gary Chapman. In this book he introduces the idea that different people express love differently. He defines the love languages as: words of affirmation, quality time, gifts, acts of service, and physical touch. Chapman says that each person has a primary and secondary love language. It's such a simple idea but was profound for me to understand that my mate may be expressing love, it just might be in a language different than my own, and therefore it may not be heard and understood. Now that we have a greater awareness of values, it's easier to see that these love languages all originate in an individual's values.

We need not value all of the same things
to be in a **healthy relationship** with another.

We do need to be aware of what they value and then respect and honor their individual perspective. There may be a few values, though, that we consider non-negotiable. With these, an overlap with your partner is essential.

This understanding surfaced for me as I re-entered the dating scene as a single woman over forty. What an education! That is a book in and of itself. I already understood that love alone was not enough to sustain a relationship. I knew there had to be some commonality of values but I hadn't dug deep into what those values were for me. I also had not considered which of my values were and were not non-negotiable.

As I sifted through my personality, connecting to others through communication was one such value that surfaced. When I ignored the absence of this value in a relationship and put other things, fun, love of music, security or adventure above it, the relationship worked for awhile but only for a short while. I came to understand that for me this was a non-negotiable. Not being able to have open and meaningful communication with my mate was completely out of alignment with my values and therefore, my nature.

When our relationship with another causes us to lack confidence and feel "needy", it may very well be that we are ignoring our values and our needs are definitely not being met. When our partner does not honor what we need in order to be self-confident, our entire foundation is shaken. Try as we may to bolster it, our value is undermined. It could be that communication regarding what we value will open our eyes and those of our partner so that we can better support each other and thus the relationship.

It is not that either person is wrong. It is that each person values specific things. When there is a values clash we often think there is something wrong with us and we just need to try harder. This is not the case. Look at what you value. Look at what the other person values. See where you overlap and where you're clashing. Are you and they willing to put the effort in to honor and be more sensitive to the other? Are you both open to respectfully support the other person's non-negotiable values? This does not mean giving "on the surface" lip service to it. It means learning to lovingly accept and support these values. If so, you have a common ground to work from. If not, neither is wrong, it just wasn't a match and you'll be a bit wiser the next time.

Determining our values affects not only our romantic relationships but also the way we connect to our lives. Once I understood how important communication was to my personality, I naturally began to live in greater alignment with authentic communication in all other areas of my life: my children, family, friends, clients and writing. This book is a result of that alignment. The tumblers fell and the vault opened.

Clarifying our values helps us to understand what brings the most fulfillments. Our values are a mirror that reflects back to us an image of who we truly are.

I've often thought of it as the process of tuning the radio to a clear station. The static that we go through is the confusion we sometimes experience about who we are. When we don't understand ourselves, either our own or others' actions cause us to be uncomfortable. We're trying to listen to the music of life but become distracted and frustrated. We're confused and spend much time questioning ourselves or wondering how we can "fix" the discomfort we feel in our relationships. Sometimes we unwittingly compromise our values in order to try to create a match. Knowing who we are and what we value clears the confusion, brings personal peace and tunes us into the joy of a life lived with clarity. This creates a very stable base for our personality. Clarity is key.

That clarity gives us many guideposts from which we can make choices. These guideposts are our values. They are imprints in our personality that when understood and applied in the events of our lives, give us a great sense of security because we are taking action that is in integrity with who we are. Brian Tracey states that values plus action equals self-confidence.

Understanding our core values propels us to **live more authentically.**

This authenticity allows others to trust their connection to us because they sense our calmness, clarity and stability. Building on the concept of service, this creates a clear path from which to serve and be served.

Determining our values is a simple yet potent process. To determine your values begin by asking yourself, "What kind of person am I?" "What has been important to me since I was young?" For example, loyalty has always been important to me. I remember as a young child being very loyal to my friends. I included my small group in everything that I did. We walked to school together, picking each one up at the corner of their street. To this day, I gladly give of my time and resources to those who have supported me. It is for this reason that I never questioned who I would work with on the cultural center project. My friend Howard and I had many spiritual conversations at Ramah Navajo School when I worked there. When the inspiration for the center was given to me, he was my only choice. He knows this and trusts me as a result. This clarity rings as true as the ping of a crystal glass.

Exercise 1

Do this exercise in complete acceptance of your individuality. Read the following list of values. Stop for a moment on each one and consider it. Pay attention to your emotions. Do you feel an emotional rise about any of them? If so, you have an emotional connection to it. When you feel that rise, listen to your thoughts and feelings. You may remember a time when that value was either very present or absent.

Speaking about loyalty, I remember being a young child and one of those friends having a birthday party but not inviting me. Why do I still remember that pain? I do because of the absence of loyalty. I bring this up so that you can think back in your life and see that if the absence of a value creates a "ping" in your memory, it's the signal of an emotional charge indicating to you what matters most.

Here's another example, you may value honesty but kept a ten-dollar bill that was given you mistakenly in a transaction. Keeping that money gave you an opportunity to see who you were and how you felt when you disregarded that value. Refrain from self-judgment but rather learn about yourself through it and understand that life is more joyful when we live by our values.

Be aware of your emotions as you read the following list. You are looking for emotional blips on the field of your consciousness. Choose each value that stands out to you.

You may want to put plus signs next to the ones that have particular impact.

When you get to the end, go back and reread your choices. Are there any that are important for you that were not on this list? Add them.

You may want to combine two or three values as long as the essential distinction doesn't change. For example you may combine honesty and truthfulness.

If you have more than eight values circled, reread your list and listen again to your "gut". Some will have more impact for you. If you find it difficult to determine your top eight, you may want to sleep on it or discuss it with someone your trust to get their perspective. Narrowing it down to your top eight values gets you to define your core. We all recognize the importance of each of the values on the list. It's essential that we determine which values are key to our individual personality.

This list was taken from "The Coaches Toolkit" in *Co-Active Coaching* by Whitworth, Kimsey-House and Sandahl.

Humor	Directness	Partnership
Productivity	Service	Contribution
Excellence	Free Sprit	Focus
Romance	Recognition	Harmony
Accomplishment	Orderliness	Forward the Action
Honesty	Success	Accuracy
Adventure	Lack of Pretense	Zest

Tradition	To Be Known	Growth
Aesthetics	Participation	Performance
Collaboration	Community	Personal Power
Freedom to Choose	Connectedness	Acknowledgment
Comradeship	Lightness	Spirituality
Empowerment	Full Self-Expression	Integrity
Creativity	Independence	Nurturing
Joy	Beauty	Authenticity
Risk Taking	Peace	Elegance
Vitality	Trust	

My top eight values are:

1._____

2._____

3._____

4._____

5._____

6._____

7._____

8._____

It would be simple to have this list of values be the end of this exercise. My desire is for you to integrate this information into your self-awareness. This level of self-knowledge takes a bit of work, but the anchoring that knowing yourself brings to your life is worth the extra effort. For this reason your next step is to take each value and write why you chose it. This will cause you to look at the roots of your values and understand their depth in your life.

Write a statement for each value that begins, "I chose this value because...."

As an example, you may respond to the value of honesty in these terms, "I chose honesty because my dad was always a very honest person and he taught me to be honest."

I cannot stress how important this next step is for you. This step caused me to create this book and launch the associated business. The spillover of this process into my life was powerful.

I want you to define each of your eight values in active terms. Remember Brian Tracy says **values + action = self-confidence.** The following question will help you define what this value means to how you live your life. Begin with the following statement and then write at least three ways that you currently or in the future will express that value.

"In terms of living my life, the ways that I express (or will express)...(put your value here) are..."

For example, "In terms of living my life, the ways that I express honesty are:

I return to others the things that belong to them.

I answer questions honestly when asked.

I am honest with myself first and foremost."

Another example, "In terms of living my life, the ways that I express love are:

I do not impose my will on another.

I accept the differences in others.

I see others and myself in their highest light.

I love myself."

Finally, look back over the three values exercises you have completed. Reread what you have written looking for the common threads that run through them. This is the essence of who you are. It is the core of your personality.

Now you're going to create a three to four sentence statement that summarizes what you value. This statement will be incredibly helpful in not only writing your purpose statement, but also guiding your life. I encourage you to write this statement on a card and read it morning and night. It is a verbal snapshot of your heart and soul. Living in alignment with it will release untold stress and add huge measures of meaning, joy and productivity to your life.

Understanding our **values** creates order in our lives.

The Universe is a very orderly place. Look at the perfection of the spiral of a conch shell or the symmetry of a clover. When we are out of order, we are out of harmony with the order that exists all around us and are therefore less effective and happy. Living in this "out of order" state causes a great deal of friction and resistance and will eventually result in crisis and disease. When we are living in alignment with what we value and the natural order of the Universe, our experience causes us to be healthy, happy and wealthy. In short, we are free to live the life we love.

These exercises are priceless tools. Use them often to help you make choices and to clarify courses of action. When you have a question as to which direction to go, ask yourself, "What is the value that I would be experiencing if I chose this action? Is it in alignment with who I am?"

Staying true to your values is an effective way to continuously reinforce your thought process towards a greater awareness of your higher nature. When we live in alignment with what we value, we experience true peace.

On a practical level, honoring your values gives you the opportunity to honor your highest nature and releases a tremendous amount of creative and motivational energy. After all, thoughts are things and are made of energy. Low-level thoughts vibrate slowly and thus slow us down, whereas thoughts of a higher nature vibrate quickly and speed us up, creating pure loving energy in our system. Think for a moment about how you feel when you're in love or when you have had a peak experience and have been "in the zone." That is what we strive to experience frequently, as we move forward in fulfilling our purpose.

Live The Life You Love

"What man actually needs
is not a tensionless state
but rather the striving and struggling
for some goal worthy of him.
What he needs is not
the discharge of tension at any cost,
but the call of a potential meaning
waiting to be fulfilled by him."

Victor **Frankl**

Chapter 4
Your Natural *Gifts* and *Talents*

> "One needs something to believe in,
> something for which one can have
> whole-hearted enthusiasm.
> One needs to feel that one's life has meaning,
> that one is needed in this world."
> Hannah **Senesh**

It is said that the formula for happiness is "Be, Do, Have." As we reflect on this formula, the foundational element of meaning and joy is "Be", which translates to an understanding of who you are and what you value. It is the base from which all experience grows.

To "be" though is only the beginning. My friend, Deborah, clarifies this very important thought beautifully, "Knowing our values and 'living' our values through the expression of our talents can be two very different stages of awareness. As we evolve in life we grow in our ability to truly live what we believe."

With this in mind, let's look at the middle word in the formula, "Do." Who we are and what we value must transfer actively through our thoughts and into our gifts and talents. How we think about anything determines how we act. Thus, living these values gives us an opportunity to act on what we believe to be most important.

To complete the above formula, part three is what we "Have". Our results are a natural outgrowth of both our thoughts and our actions.

In terms of the Navajo culture project, the "be" part is what I value: culture, personal development, spiritual awareness, being of service and authenticity. The "do" portion of this formula involves using my talents in verbal communication, writing, imagination and leadership to create the vision and funding for the cultural learning center. The "have" portion manifests in the creation of the Hogan, the booking of guests and the empowering of the cultural and healing programs.

Connecting our **values** to our **talents** and **gifts** gives us a chance **to live** what we believe to be **important.**

It is also through our talents that we translate our purpose into action.

Your gifts and talents are as individual as your values. One of the great paradoxes of life is to understand just how unique each of us is while also understanding that we are all fundamentally the same. Like the uniqueness of a snowflake, each one that falls has a different crystal pattern, a different personality, but...each one is still snow, composed of the same essential elements.

Your ***purpose*** involves both your overt and covert ***strengths*** and ***talents***.

Although some are rather quiet in expression, they are very much present. It may be interesting for you to know that writing was a covert talent of mine. I was an art education major in college, with an emphasis in painting. After I began teaching I wanted to continue to paint, so I set up my studio and launched a small art business. As I look back, I didn't see myself as having a talent in writing. I earned good grades in English but I always saw myself as an artist. Everyone around me did too.

This covert talent didn't surface until I began pondering my values and purpose. It was a natural outgrowth of my desire to bring my thoughts on personal development to the forefront. At that point, my biggest hurdle to writing a book was that although I had a quiet talent in writing, I didn't see myself as an author. I wrestled with this bigger image of myself but the thought of writing a book wouldn't leave me alone. It whispered, then called and finally shouted. All kinds of evidence fell into my life showing me that I had more talent in this area than I thought. I grabbed on to this feedback, building a store of evidence that finally toppled the limiting belief. This is why it's imperative that you look at all of your strengths and talents, even the ones that barely whisper.

Passions ignite us at the core.

Your passions are also a good indicator in determining your purpose. Webster defines passion as "A strong liking or desire for, or devotion to some activity, object, or concept." The things we're passionate about are divine sparks that fuel our life. Passions grow out of our devotion to our values. It's surprising though that some passions are allowed to spend a lifetime asleep. Because of the emotional nature of passions, they have incredible inspirational and motivational energy. It is said that our heart or emotions are our spiritual connection with God. With this being the case unleashing our passions releases us to a greater connection with the Divine.

It comes as no surprise to you that I have a passion for communication. It compelled me to learn the Italian language fairly quickly when I moved to Italy and lived with an Italian family for six months. It drove me crazy that I was reduced to the point of being able to express myself in one word sentences with the help of my Italian/English dictionary. That same passion took me into the world of teaching, facilitating seminars and now writing.

This book is very much an on-purpose project for me. It gives me a chance to express my passion for teaching, my talent for communicating and my love for helping others. The catalyst then was mixing this formula with a compulsion to write.

Many have been raised to believe that recognition of something good in us is boastful and brash. I hope that through these pages you can see that recognition of our talents allows us to live more joyfully and in better service to humanity. Maintaining this alignment keeps us very humble. Our focus is not ourselves but others.

Allow yourself to recognize what you do well and what you love to do. All of this information about you creates flashes of self-awareness, that when the illumination is connected, the image emerges.

This next exercise will be amazingly valuable for you. Take time to do it now because your conscious mind is open

to the suggestion of your sub-conscious mind. You are in the perfect frame of mind to receive inspiration. Skipping it would be like being too busy driving to stop for gas. In the end, it will slow your progress miserably.

Write your answers to some questions about yourself, your gifts and talents. Sit in a peaceful, quiet place and reflect. The questions are simple yet when approached thoughtfully, the insights can be profound. The gift or talent you write about need not be confined to only those pursuits that seem altruistic or are focused on philanthropic service to humanity. It can involve a talent in finances, real estate, teaching, business, speaking, athletics, etc. How you will use these talents is the altruistic part of this process. We'll get to that.

If you find it difficult to write about your talents ask someone close to you to help give you perspective on yourself. A friend or an interviewer can be effective in assisting you to discover some of your hidden talents. Sometimes people are raised to think that talking about the things that they do well is conceited. However, understanding our gifts allows us greater opportunity to use them in service to others. You may opt to do this in addition to your own perspectives even if you are comfortable writing about yourself. Feedback from others is very helpful.

- ❂ "What do you love to do? (Personally, professionally, socially)
- ❂ "What is it, that when you are doing it, you lose track of time?"
- ❂ "What are your passions that give your life depth and meaning?"
- ❂ "What are your talents, skills or special aptitudes that you can use in service to the world?"
- ❂ "What have been your past successes in business, community service, etc?"
- ❂ "What would people say are your greatest strengths?"

Describe a peak experience.

On his website, Robert Knowlton, purpose coach, outlines the "Top 10 Steps for Defining your Personal Purpose." He encourages his clients to answer similar questions regarding their strengths and talents and then suggests they group their answers into like categories.

Once grouped, he has them put a heading on each category describing the natural talent that they possess that is the general theme of each grouping. The examples Robert uses are: "see the big picture" or "able to elicit trust" or "spatially visualize mechanical structure."

As an example, as I worked through this process with one client who was a dentist, he found it difficult to see the patterns in his values. As we discussed his responses I saw that he had a love for recognition and being in center stage. He also valued making a big impact in people's lives. I began to see a pattern and although he had never done any public speaking prior to our coaching, I could see that doing some type of speaking would be very fulfilling for him. He was thrilled by the prospect and the resulting self-knowledge that simply knowing and honoring this about him brought.

It is this type of pattern you are looking for. Seeing the patterns emerge in our personality creates a powerful understanding of who we are at very fundamental levels. This understanding, when integrated, causes us to consciously create specific actions that are in alignment with our values. There is nothing that will clear chaos from life like living in alignment with your values.

I like this step. Grouping your responses allows you to take the information you have just written and begin to see patterns in it. These patterns are huge indicators that offer clarity regarding who you are. I also believe that it gives you the broad categories to live by. The self-knowledge you are gaining right now is priceless. You'll bring far more of yourself to the game of life when you know who you are and what your talents and gifts are.

Think about entering the professional world with this knowledge. You'd choose a better professional match, do a more insightful job filling out an application or creating a resume and you'd give a far better interview, I'm certain of it.

Once you understand these patterns, you'll also be better able to carry this newly acquired self-knowledge into all the areas of your life.

Take time to do this pattern exercise now.

✪   ✪   ✪   ✪   ✪

In this part of the process, you will consider the service you give to others. Doing this will lead you seamlessly into discovering your purpose. Think in terms of the ways the talents, passions and skills listed above can benefit others. Ask yourself how you can co-create a life situation where the things that you love to do can become a bigger part of your life and be of service to others. Write your thoughts concerning these questions. This can be a simple collection of thoughts and ideas.

The awareness that this process has created in your marvelous mind will set the creative wheels turning. Leave a pad and pen by your bedside to "download" more ideas as they come. Many wealthy people constantly carry a pocket pad or piece of folded paper with them to capture ideas when inspiration delivers them. Don't let them slip by, thinking that you'll remember. You'll find yourself frustrated and trying to think back to the idea that flew through your creative mind. I remember an old rancher telling me once, "A dull pencil remembers better than a sharp mind." That's a bit of cowboy wisdom.

Keep these ideas handy, as we'll be using them to determine your purpose.

This entire chapter has been about **discovery**.

As you read these last lines, I'm certain you know yourself much better. The process of recognizing your gifts and talents is a very big exercise for some.

Take this knowledge about you and allow it to support your understanding that you came here to develop, express and enjoy your personality as you deliver your unique gifts and talents to the world. Allow this self-knowledge to steady you when you need strength and to guide you when you need direction. Know that the development of these talents will give you incredible joy as you touch your highest nature.

As I write this, I think of the Olympians that represent our countries. They are a perfect example of the value of developing gifts and talents. Through the sublime experience of the expression of their passion, they bring honor to their countries and provide inspirational examples of the heights ordinary people can reach through focus, discipline and right thought. You are on a quest to do the same through the magnificent expression of your purpose.

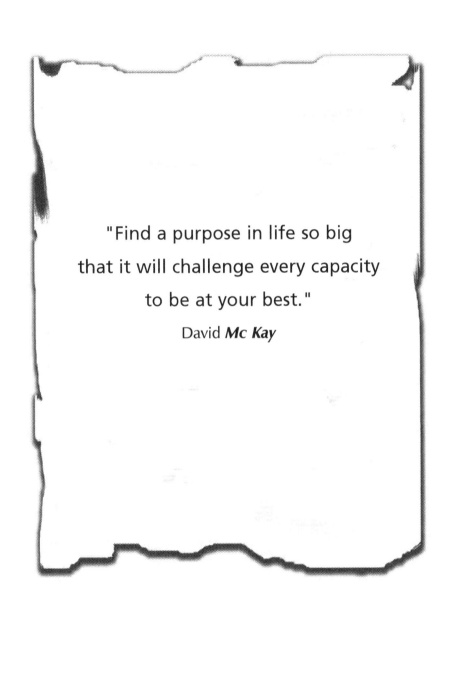

"Find a purpose in life so big
that it will challenge every capacity
to be at your best."

David *Mc Kay*

Chapter 5

Writing Your *Purpose* Statement

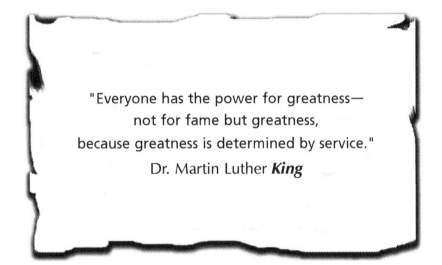

"Everyone has the power for greatness—
not for fame but greatness,
because greatness is determined by service."
Dr. Martin Luther **King**

You have identified your values, talents, strengths and passions. Now it's time to try your hand at writing your purpose statement. I'll be right here to walk you through the process. I have a very simple step-by-step plan. I want to reassure you that your first attempt is only a draft. You'll write it several times as you work through the process. It will evolve. Each interaction with writing your purpose will cause you to think deeply about what gives your life meaning and joy.

During the writing and rewriting of your early drafts don't be concerned with the final product, simply get your ideas down on paper. Once you come up with a purpose statement that you feel comfortable with and inspired by, live with it for a while. See if it stands the test of time. If it does, great, if it doesn't, that's great too. Purpose statements, like good relationships, take time and focused attention.

Your purpose statement should be concise, no more than a few sentences. This statement is the essence of how you choose to live your life. It is how you approach each moment of each day and will become the compass with which you navigate. Your purpose statement is your *true north*. It should be simple so that you remember it, yet powerful so that it guides you. An active and energetic statement will strike at the very core of you and compel you to live to your greatest potential.

This statement will save you huge amounts of time, money and frustration. I've had many opportunities to be involved in a variety of business projects since I left teaching. Many looked very profitable and interesting. At one point I was even talking to a developer about creating an airstrip and traditional time-share properties at my ranch. None of this felt quite right. Why? It was all off-purpose for me or only intersected with my purpose intermittently. I would have had to invest a tremendous amount of extra effort and energy to cause myself to stay focused and excited about a project that wasn't a good fit for me.

I know you can feel my excitement and passion regarding both the cultural center project and the writing of this book. I'm so glad I've done the work that I have on determining my purpose. I could have easily been sidetracked and missed this opportunity to more fully experience my self.

The plan is to create a life where resistance is minimal and where we're living from the values and talents that enliven us and give us incredible joy. The projects that we build will take effort. There will be challenges to solve. We want to be so connected with the vision and the joy of creating that any challenge seems like a little bump on the super-highway of your life.

The effort I'm expending on the New Mexico project is sizable but as I give the project what it needs I feel like I'm part of an amazing adventure and one step closer to an incredible contribution.

Let's talk about what your purpose statement is not. It's not a goal statement. As I mentioned earlier, each moment that we live in love, kindness and service to another we are living on purpose, however harmony with others is only a small piece of purposeful living. Living in harmony is more of a goal for joyful living. It is not necessary to write purpose statements for actions of kindness, love, generosity and service unless you have set these as a specific intention. They are ways of life.

As I conducted research for this book, I found several sites with examples of what they felt were purpose statements. A statement such as, "It is my purpose to get along better with my neighbors" is not a life's purpose statement. It is a statement of intent to live an individual's values more fully. Writing and living by a statement such as this is foundational but only one facet of living a purposeful life. It is like one color on one section of a beach ball. It's important but not the whole picture.

I also found resources that broke down the writing of a purpose statement into categories such as, personal, spiritual, vocational and relational, or society, family, body/wellness, finances, and spiritual/religious. I believe these categories are helpful in creating clarity and focus for purposeful living, but creating categorical statements for each area segments our purpose and therefore creates more of a specific goal statement. We are integrated human beings, and as such bring all of who we are to every aspect of our lives. A life's purpose statement creates focus and direction for all areas of your life.

Going back to the *"be, do, have"* formula, this is the *"be"* part. Who are you as you take action in all areas of your life? Why are you here? As an example, mine is, "I use my resources and talents to support people of all cultures and backgrounds to live purposeful, joyful and successful lives and to gain increased global understanding."

As you read my statement you can see that I am entirely "on purpose" by developing my ranch as a cultural retreat center and by writing and publishing this book. I completely lose track of time when I'm working on these projects. They both bring me incredible joy, meaning and fulfillment. Working on these purposeful projects has caused me to grow in ways I couldn't have imagined and to meet people I'm so grateful to have met. As I've worked to gain support for the Oso Vista Ranch project, I've had the opportunity to speak with state senators, state representatives, cabinet secretaries and tribal leaders. There have been times when I've been very nervous about stepping through a door in to this unfamiliar territory. The vision of this dream has inspired me to "step up" to the challenge, overcome my fears and talk to whoever would listen to my dream. As I've left these meetings, where the support has been overwhelming, I have grown in self-respect. That is the priceless side-benefit that purposeful living delivers with regularity. Our purpose is that mission which calls us to a larger experience of our potential.

All of that said, let's get started on writing your purpose statement. As we begin, it is very important for you to understand that we are thinking forward to the full expression of your essence, your talents, and your passions. This is not a statement of what you have accomplished or who you are at this point. Your purpose will draw you to growth. Allow your mind to be open to new possibilities.

Just as the dentist uncovered that he'd absolutely love to express his values related to public speaking, you may be itching to express talents in a new direction. You do not need to be accomplished already at the purpose you describe here. It is a destination you are defining. Don't allow past limiting beliefs to be a part of this process. You're a powerful creator...create the point you are sailing to.

David Gordon and Graham Dawes developed an excellent formula for writing a purpose statement (expandyourworld.net). They succinctly break the purpose statement down into four parts: Essential Action, Central Concern, Beneficiary, and Intended Impact. Robert Knowlton (SuccessOptions.com) has built upon this work. It is Robert's expansion of this work that is the basis for this next process.

First, they say that a purpose statement has an essential action. This action is how you intend to engage with the world. This statement uses your talents and gifts as a foundation and focuses on how you will actively deliver the service you intend to give. In my statement this concept translates to: "I use my resources and my talents..." You may state this in whatever way speaks to you. Remember this is the "essential action" portion of the statement. Write it in the present tense.

To help you, I've chosen a few examples from people's lives that are and have lived passionate dreams. Feel free to model any of these statements that fit for you.

Think of Albert Einstein. Without question, he lived a purposeful life. His essential action may have been "to use his brilliant mind."

Switching fields to athletics, think about Tiger Woods. Stop for a moment and think about what you suppose his purpose is. I have been touched by watching his personal discipline in developing his golf talents to a level never reached before. I see him as one who accesses the Infinite through his game. I look at his face on the cover of Sports Illustrated and his ability to focus entirely in the moment inspires me. So, I suppose that his essential action may be "to use his focus, imagination, athleticism and personal leadership in golf." He has been an inspiration to people of every background, culture and race.

Take an athlete like Lance Armstrong. At the writing of this book he has captured his seventh Tour de France title. I believe his essential action is "to use his mental and physical discipline, his unstoppable drive and his athletic ability in cycling." He has brought cycling to a new level and infused it with heart and soul.

Another obvious example of a purpose driven life is Mother Theresa. She says her purpose is "to see Jesus Christ in every human being that she comes in contact with." She engages with the world through her ability to see the highest light in all things.

Consider the well-known Oprah Winfrey from the business and entertainment arena. She is a great example of a woman living a life of resilience and service. Despite her impressive business savvy, what I respect even more is her humble beginnings. Her story honors the same dream within each of us: the desire to reach beyond our challenges and live our greatest potential. The action through which she engages with her purpose may be, "By example and through service, creativity and excellence." The list of superlatives for Oprah's contributions could be quite lengthy.

Take time now to draft part one.

Step number two in the process is to determine your central concern. The purpose of this part is to delineate what your attention or action is focused on creating. This portion of your purpose statement defines what you will do/produce, given the essential action.

What will I use my talents to do? Looking at my statement, the answer would be, "To support..."

Now think about Einstein. What did he use his brilliant mind to do? It may have been "to stretch the mental capacity."

For both athletes and admirers Tiger Woods has created a far bigger vision of the game of golf and how it can be taken to a level of perfection that absolutely inspires all of us to develop our own greatness. We see the fruits of his work and sacrifice as we watch him funnel that passion into perfection. So, for him it may be "to inspire greatness."

Oprah has contributed significantly to the celebration of women. Watching her show and reading her magazine has inspired women around the world to create healthier bodies, minds and spirits. She is a powerful example of excellence in business. I believe her central concern is service and her material gain is simply a by-product of that service. Therefore, I suppose her central concern to be quite direct, "To positively impact, educate, and inspire."

Mother Theresa worked "to give medical, physical and spiritual relief."

Lance has brought hope to cancer survivors in a way we'll never forget. The world has united in support of his vision. For Lance it may be, "to bring hope and inspiration."

Take your essential action and add your central concern to it.

Let's move on to step three of the purpose writing process. Knowlton says that you must have a beneficiary. This is "who" you intend to touch through your service. This needs less explanation but it's essential that you get very clear on whom you desire to benefit. In marketing this is determining your target audience.

In mine, I desire to have a far reach and to touch people of all cultures and backgrounds in large and small ways. I want to positively impact the checker at the grocery store, an individual coaching client on the phone and the person who sits down with a cup of tea and my book. Therefore, I state it this way, "people of all cultures and backgrounds..."

This is a far more concrete portion of the statement although, I caution you to really think about it. Who do you want to impact? With public people like Einstein, Woods, Armstrong, Mother Theresa and Oprah it is easy to see that their lives touch all those who experience or witness their contributions.

More specifically though, Einstein showed how science and spirituality are different personalities of the same creative essence. By tapping both, he left the world changed. So Einstein touched "humanity."

With Woods, he has been an example of excellence in golf "to all people."

Mother Theresa focused her attention on "the slums of the world," and in so doing she brought the example of compassion to us all.

For Armstrong perhaps the greatest beneficiaries have been "those with or who have been affected by cancer and illness of all types." It didn't stop there though, because his story of overcoming has been inspirational for the world. When we are in the presence of greatness, we are forever changed.

With Oprah, although her reach has touched people of all cultures, customs, and genders, she especially inspires "women worldwide."

Who do YOU want to touch? Define this now and add it to your essential action and central concern.

Lastly, Knowlton says there must be an intended impact. What is the outcome you desire to achieve? What do you desire your service to result in? As an example, mine closes with, "To live purposeful, joyful and successful lives and to gain increased global understanding."

Einstein's intended impact may be to help people "consider new possibilities and create order in their understanding of the forces of nature."

For Woods it could be to inspire people everywhere "to push their personal limits through focused discipline to create peak experiences in sports and life."

For Oprah it might be to positively impact women worldwide "to live happier, healthier lives as they grow to their greatest potential." The fact that she profits handsomely from giving this service is completely in alignment with the laws of giving and receiving, for Oprah gives greatly. She has learned to maximize this law. It is a part of her potent example for living.

For Mother Theresa it could be "to alleviate suffering and bring wellness and comfort." Her humble work touched us all.

With Armstrong I experience a message of "overcoming adversity and living fully the adventure of life."

This simple formula demystifies the writing process and covers all the bases.

Stop and add your intended impact to the end of your statement.

❂　❂　❂　❂　❂

Here are the sample purpose statements, which I have supposed, for the people above:

Einstein

To use his brilliant mind to stretch the mental capacity of humanity so that they may consider new possibilities and create order in their understanding of the forces of nature.

Woods

To use his focus, imagination, athleticism and personal leadership in golf to inspire all people to push past their personal limits through focused discipline and create peak experiences in sports and life.

Armstrong

To use mental and physical discipline, unstoppable drive and athletic ability in cycling to bring hope and inspiration to those affected by cancer and illness, to overcome adversity and live fully the adventure of life.

Mother Teresa

To use her ability to see Jesus Christ in every human being, giving medical, physical and spiritual relief to the poor in the slums of the world by alleviating suffering and bringing wellness and comfort.

Oprah

By example and through service, creativity and excellence, she positively impacts, educates and inspires women worldwide to live happier, healthier lives as they grow to their greatest potential.

While talking about this book with my friend Connie Kadanski, owner of Exceptional Sales Performance, she reminded me that a purpose statement might change with time, "As you grow in self-awareness, your purpose will grow with you. You may find that you revise it to reflect a greater depth of understanding." I agree. The purpose statement you begin drafting today may change as your self-awareness changes or it may not. Its essence, though, will carry through to any new writings.

If you haven't stopped to create your purpose statement yet, consider yourself busted!

Resist your desire to read this like a novel and take some time right now to work on your statement. Your mind is in alignment with this material, which makes this the best time for you to try your hand at writing it. You may write several different versions and then see which one best suits you over time. Stay open to the fact that defining your purpose in writing is a process that takes time. It is time well invested.

I remember a story That Stephen Covey tells about a crew of workers clearing a road through a forest. A visionary leader climbed a tree and after getting his bearings calls down to the crew, "Stop! Wrong forest!"

The manager yells back up, "Be quiet! We're making progress!" Know that you can work day after day, wearying yourself with empty "progress" because you're in the wrong forest. Stop; reorient your life's energy to the right forest.

In review, the four parts are: Essential Action (how you will actively deliver the service you intend to give), Central Concern (delineate what your attention or action is focused on creating), Beneficiary (who you intend to benefit), and Intended Impact (what impact you intend to create).

When you have done sufficient work on this step, move on. We're about to explore how to integrate your purpose into your life.

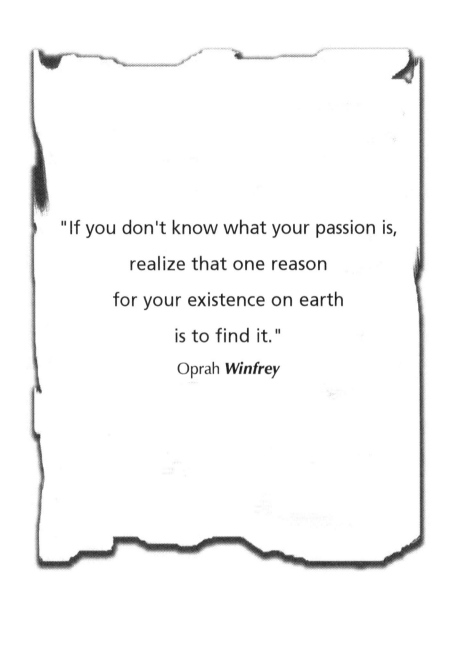

"If you don't know what your passion is,

realize that one reason

for your existence on earth

is to find it."

Oprah **Winfrey**

Live The Life You Love

Chapter 6

The *Power* of Words

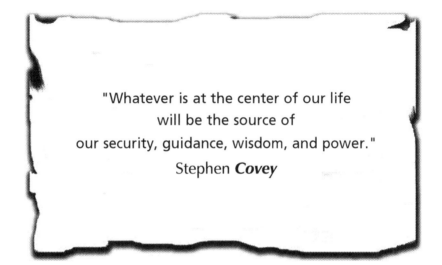

"Whatever is at the center of our life
will be the source of
our security, guidance, wisdom, and power."

Stephen **Covey**

Now that you have a purpose statement, how do you turn it into action? How do you allow it to guide your life and attain what the Buddhists call *Right Livelihood*?

The next step is for you to develop a vision of what you are creating.

Your purpose is the "why." Your vision is the "what." Your goal is the "how". God, Infinite Intelligence, the Universe gives us free will to express ourselves and our purpose in whatever way we choose. Choice is a significant aspect of living our purpose.

We choose our path. Although all paths lead to learning, some lead more quickly to greater awareness and expedite the experience of happiness in our lives. Living on-purpose is one such path. It reduces the drama by keeping us on course.

Developing a clear vision statement is a very effective way of communicating with the Infinite to co-create our lives, as we desire them to be. Infinite Intelligence always provides us with the experiences we ask for. Our purpose and vision statements give us an avenue with which to communicate our desires. It is through this contact that we access our power to live the vision that we create.

The vision statement empowers us by allowing us to take complete responsibility for our lives. We are stating from the start how we desire our lives and results to be...in detail. It is primarily an acknowledgment of our Creator and our co-creative abilities because it is based on the idea that what we visualize we can create. An understanding of this one thought can shift your life forever. An Infinitely Intelligent power created each of us and has only our highest good in mind. We have access to this creative power every moment of every day. We choose its help by emotionally speaking our desires through our purpose, vision and intentional goals.

As Tony Burroughs says, "All who step forth, with trust and love in their hearts are answered. The Universe wants you to know your power. It wants you to have it all. Indeed, it longs to stop your suffering and waits for the moment when you will approach life in earnest so that it can show you the fullest expression of yourself."

Fully engaging with our purpose and then creating our vision is absolutely essential. This is where we're creating the vision of the path that will express our purpose. This can be a bit unnerving in the beginning as we're clueless as to how we're going to create that vision. It's okay. We'll focus on the how in a bit. For now, write this as if you cannot fail. Believe in my belief in you and this process.

Do know that I understand. It takes a tremendous amount of courage to commit to a dream. I remember writing my letter of resignation to the Ramah Navajo School Board. It was both liberating and unnerving. I knew it was necessary though, because as I stayed where it was safe and familiar my potential and dreams were shrinking a day at a time. Above all, I believed in the vision I held for my life and clung to the purpose that compelled me.

Let's get very clear on what your *vision statement* is.

It is the expansion of your purpose statement. It helps you begin to unfold your picture of what you intend to create as you live your purpose. The purpose is the blueprint; the vision is the architect's drawing; the intentional goal is the building of the project.

My purpose, "I use my resources and talents to support people of all cultures and backgrounds to live purposeful, joyful and successful lives and gain increased global understanding."

My vision, "We have created the mental and physical environments through "Live The Life You Love" and Oso Vista Ranch for the global and Ramah Navajo Communities to experience healing, personal growth, purpose development and increased global understanding. We give people more than they expect through providing the most authentic, thoughtful and meaningful experiences possible, a comfortable and well-maintained venue, valuable seminars, life-changing coaching, and on-going support. In return we are compensated with thriving businesses and abundant profits."

The vision of what you will manifest through your purpose may very well involve dreams you have already dreamed and projects you have in process.

This book and Oso Vista have been in process for years. Even before I could see the clear vision, I had a hazy feeling that my life and Oso Vista had a greater purpose. As I grew, it was the book that first began whispering to me. It took a while for me to grow in confidence enough to allow that whisper to speak. When it wouldn't leave me alone, I decided that if I was to be a writer, I must write. It was choppy at first but I was determined. The more I wrote, the better I got. The better I got, the more I grew.

It was only after I had grown to this point that the vision of the land could begin to manifest in my imagination. Because of my success with writing, I had a greater capacity to believe in my abilities, therefore my imagination was more open to suggestion.

The same will be true for you. There have been whispers in your heart that long to see the light of day. They compel you to grow so that they can manifest into the physical world. Up until now they may have been unsettling because you didn't understand why they wouldn't let you go. Now you understand their purpose. These whispers were your unconscious attempts to live your purpose. It's time to act upon them consciously.

Your **purpose** and **vision**,
once empowered by your **awareness**,
will pull you through tough spots,
give your life **direction** during times of great growth
and provide **focus** to your days by
reminding you of "the big picture."

Find people who are also working on creating a greater destiny and meet with them regularly so that you can support each other. Remember, in terms of masterminding an idea, one plus one equals three because of the synergy that is created between you.

Bob Proctor, friend and mentor, says of vision, "Your vision that you are mentally entertaining must always be clear, larger and more magnificent than the controlling conditions or circumstances which you presently find yourself surrounded by in your material world. It is the vision in your mind harmonizing with your purpose, which creates the inspiration that causes you to stretch."

The critical link between your purpose and your daily intentions or goals lies in your vision. Intentions are the actions you take to live your purpose and manifest your vision. To state this clearly, purpose is the *why*, vision is the *what* and your goals or intention are the *how*. This simple formula guided me through my process of creating a clearly defined direction for the life change I underwent.

Don't skip this step because defining your vision will begin to give you the details that will lead you to the *how* part of the equation.

As James Allen in *As A Man Thinketh* says, "The vision that you glorify in your mind, the ideal that you enthrone in your heart; this you will build your life by, and this you will become."

Exercise 4

Write your purpose statement on the top of a piece of paper. Relax and open your mind to inspiration and possibilities. If you find past limiting beliefs surfacing, gently release them and replace them with confidence that you are creating a new path for your life and old fears and limits are just shadows of another day.

Then brainstorm, either alone or with a friend, all of the ways you could realize that purpose. Open your mind and do not judge your ideas. You may have an inspirational thought that you have never before considered. Include projects, ideas or businesses that would give you a creative outlet for your talents and passions. Don't worry about how you will create them. Simply allow the ideas to arrive without judgment. Remember, inspiration and possibilities. Allow brand new ideas to be born.

Think of projects or businesses you have experienced in the past, are currently working on, or have always wanted to create that are expressions of these talent, passions and gifts. Write them down. This list is only the beginning. As you remain open to ideas, you will be amazed at how many possibilities will come to you. Put a pad and paper by your bed because the relaxed state of sleep opens creative channels that the conscious mind clouds.

Next, take a look at this list and choose the ones that you feel excited about or are most interested in. Listen to your feelings. Which ones feel most positive to you? Your emotional connection to an idea is a clue as to its creative potential in your life. Our days should be filled with the things that bring us joy and meaning. Pick the ones that enliven you, which pick your spirit up to think about.

Remember you are focusing on what you want to create with your purpose. Think possibilities. Do not allow your ego to step in and tell you that your ideas won't work or that you're being foolish to think of doing such a thing. This part of the process is not about how. Also, remember that growing into our purpose causes us to stretch, develop new talents and experience more of our potential than we have ever known. If you already know how to create the things you are envisioning, you may not be thinking big enough. Time to get completely out of the box.

❂ ❂ ❂ ❂ ❂

Now begin your vision statement with the powerful words, "I" or "I am..." Focus on what you want to create with your purpose. Keep yourself from getting into how you'll make it all happen.

You may find that the first statement that you write is quite long. This is fine. Sometimes it takes a bit of imaginative wandering in order to get the substance flowing. You can then go back and distill it to some essential ingredients that really excite you. It will be longer than your purpose statement but should be no longer than a paragraph or two.

Some well-placed descriptors help to create a greater emotional connection between you and the statement. Our sub-conscious mind is emotional in nature. It is our heart center and our link to Universal Intelligence or God. When we speak to our sub-conscious in an emotional language, the potency creates a stronger connection between our Creator and us. Small addition...huge results.

Another reason for creating a statement that has emotional impact is that it's one of the two ways to create change. We have all heard people say, "I had an emotional experience that caused me to change my life." Creating emotional impact in our statement helps to facilitate movement toward our vision. Movement is an act of faith that infuses the process with power.

Take time now, while you are in complete alignment with these ideas, to create your vision. Include plenty of emotion and detail so that it inspires you. Let the ideas flow freely.

Remember, there are no wrong **answers**.

"A life purpose statement
is another way to
capture the essence of what it means
to be fully alive.
To be living intentionally,
to be making choices that increase the
value of life to self and others,
is a description of
being fulfilled today and every day."

Co-Active Coaching

Whitworth, Kimsey-House and Sandahl

Chapter 7

What Is *Intention*?

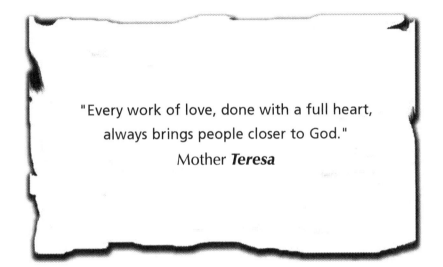

> "Every work of love, done with a full heart,
> always brings people closer to God."
>
> Mother *Teresa*

$\mathcal{J}$ have been a goal setter all of my life. I image a final result and then go to work to spiritually and creatively manifest it in my life. Although to a large degree this process has worked, I now understand that it lacked the power and inspired connection present in intentional living. This chapter will help you to see how living intentionally is the goal setting process empowered and infused with the divine brilliance of your co-creative bond with God.

Let's talk first about *goals*.

Setting and reaching goals is a common process. I have helped hundreds of people set goals. I find that the results depend as much on the personality of the person working through the process as anything. Harv Ecker says that how we do anything is how we do everything. I have found this statement to be an absolute truth.

If the person setting the goal is focused, their goal setting and achieving process will also be focused. If the person is spiritual, the process will include the Infinite. If they are confused, their approach will be confusing and chaotic. If they lack confidence, their process will be riddled with spurts of progress and then mental backslides.

When people are judgmental, they judge through the entire process. They begin by judging the goal according to what others may think of it and as a result, think of them. I have seen people set goals to impress their mentor or their friends as if the value of the goal gives them more worth. When the goal setting process is tied to the individual and their personality, it is inherently limited and often filled with human drama.

I have also seen that if for some reason a person who allows ego to define their goal-setting deadline does not reach their goal, they feel shame and guilt. They wonder what is wrong with them and why they cannot reach goals. As a result, they feel valueless. This is so far from the truth.

The problem here is not with goals, just as the issue with money is not the money itself. The essence of the goal setting process is healthy and valuable because it causes us to grow to more of our potential. The issue here is whether we choose the goal setting process to be ego or divinely driven.

Dr. Wayne Dyer says that when we let personal ego determine our direction in life we unplug ourselves from the Divine help that is available to us upon request.

He defines six ego beliefs that cause separation from others, from inspiration and from Spirit. In summary, they are: what I own and what I do defines my value, how others see me defines who I am, I am alone and unconnected from others, I am disconnected from everything I desire and I am separate from God.

The above beliefs rule the lives of many people. Living with these ego beliefs as the defining factor in life would be as shaky as building our Hogan without a foundation. The monsoon rains that flood the desert mountains would cause it to quickly settle and sink until it would be nothing but a pile of logs in a mud puddle. Great care is being given to our construction methods so that we have a Hogan that will not only look good but will last. When we define ourselves by exterior factors, we give power over our happiness to these external forces.

An internal locus of control is the prime personality trait of healthy individuals. This terminology is used frequently in self-esteem work with teens. I first learned about the value of this concept when I was working with a Youth Leadership Project headed by a long-time friend of mine who is a Cherokee Indian. His projects funded facilitators to do experiential wilderness and leadership training with teens to help them see that they are confident, empowered human beings who make healthy decisions regarding their lives. His research showed that when an individual learns that their power is within, they have the confidence to resist drugs, alcohol and any other self-depreciating behavior.

In the work we are doing here, defining and living by your values causes you to develop this internal locus or live from the center out. When an individual knows and loves who they are, they know their value is internal, that others do not define them, and that they are connected to others, to their dreams and to God.

Values are deeply rooted in *higher principles*.

Because of their altruistic nature, values cause us to raise our thoughts and thus our actions far above ego gratification. It's a brilliant plan that has been placed in our hearts.

Think again of Hawkins' map of consciousness from one to 1000. Inspiration and creation exceed 500 on the scale. As we move into higher and higher levels of thought, we come into an awareness of the oneness of all things. It is through the values of love, creation, acceptance, solution, and a host of others, that we find that we are all one heart, all one mind, and all one spirit. This is "Oneness." Our individual personality simply adds spice to the mix.

When we tune in to Infinite Intelligence in this way, we experience oneness with each other, the planet and God.

Pure, accepting, cooperative, free flowing, loving energy fully demonstrates the spirit of the Infinite.

As I taught for over twenty years in the Ramah Navajo community I began to feel such oneness with the "Dine" that I forgot that I was from a different background. As I looked out on to the world from my perspective, I felt an amazing connection with my friends and students. I remember washing my hands in the Wal-Mart bathroom at the middle of three sinks. On my left and right were traditional Navajo women. I looked up into the mirror and was taken aback at how different I looked from them. My spirit had reached such a place of connection that I had forgotten all differences. My friend, Howard, still teases me about being the blonde haired, blue eyed one.

Let's add another thought to this concept of **Oneness**.

God is also creative in nature. As we look around ourselves, we see evidence of creation everywhere. Understanding the creative nature of God is essential to grasping the manifestation process.

The next leap is an understanding that if you are an individualized spark of God and God is creative, then you are also creative in nature. Have you ever wondered why you have been so compelled to expand your life? This is why. We are all expressions of Spirit and as Bob Proctor often says, "Spirit is always for expansion and fuller expression."

This is the single most important key in the intentional manifestation process. If we believe that it is up to us to muscle over our goals, we will only bring about what we can muster alone.

People enmeshed in goal setting as an ego-driven, controlled process are always busy, maxed-out, living on the edge of constant overwhelm, and feel tired and frustrated with no time to stop and enjoy the journey. They have too much to do in too little time and nobody helps them enough. Sadly, they miss the daily peace and sweetness of life that comes from partnership with the Creator.

Think of how much more we can create and with such ease, when we come to an understanding that we aren't alone in this creative process.

This single concept multiplies your potential. It is no longer you + your goals = your results. It is now God and you + your goals + the power of intention = inspired results. These two formulas live in different realms. One is earthbound and the other limitless.

So how is it that we must be in **order** for us to live in **alignment** with our nature as **intentional creators**?

Dyer explains the seven faces of intention in his book, *The Power of Intention*. He says we must be creative, kind and loving, see the beauty in all things, be always working to expand our potential, see the abundance in all things, and trust God's Divine pace.

Choosing to live this way keeps us in alignment with God. Since God is infinitely creative, as we maintain alignment we access our own infinite creativity.

Now that we have talked about the power of connecting with Spirit in this creative process, let's get practical. Words are the first level of physical creation. Your written purpose and vision statements are more powerful than you and I could ever know. You have shaped a written prototype with these statements. It's time to manifest that prototype in the physical world.

The **"how"** of this process
is the final mental **planning step**.

Take your vision statement and consider "how" you will physically create it. What do you want your end result to look like? You may need to brainstorm some possible businesses or projects that will bring you to this result. Allow your purpose and vision to guide you. Resist your inclination to fall in to thinking what's possible. That is ego driven and completely out of sync with what you have learned. Be inspired and know that you are in creative partnership with God. That completely blows the lid off all possibility. Write everything down.

When I had first determined my purpose, it read, "I use my resources and talents to support people of all cultures and backgrounds to live purposeful, joyful and successful lives and to gain increased global understanding." The possibilities of how I could do this were endless.

As I grew, I knew a book and Oso Vista were in the plan. That was when I developed my first vision statement. At that point I didn't have a clearly defined idea. It was sketchy. If you have an inkling of a project, write it down.

I also knew I wanted to both e-publish and print publish. I wrote those ideas down. I knew I needed a website, programs and products. I wrote that down. I knew I needed to do some renovations on the retreat center. I listed those and anything else that came to me.

If you have brainstormed a list of projects, take a look at them and see if some lead up to a final, big idea. Mine includes the building of individual Hogans for people to stay in at Oso Vista Ranch while they do purpose discovery or personal development work and have the opportunity to authentically experience Navajo culture. We're still working toward that goal. I hold the vision of it daily as I support the building of the first ceremonial structure.

Often the achievement of a "big goal" will cause you to have achieved other smaller goals along the way. Sometimes the smaller goals will flex as your perspective flexes. This is an organic process and will grow naturally with your focused care.

Read back through the list and see how many of the ideas you are interested in following up on. Remove them from the list. It's good you allowed yourself to be creative. Now you can discard any ideas that you have no interest in.

As in my case you may wind up with several projects you desire to launch. There is probably one that you will see as being the initial step or goal. Write down a brief description of this result.

It's naturally time to determine when you'd like to create this first goal. Remember when you begin to set your time line that as you visualize the completion of your goals, you will be getting help from people, places and things that you haven't even connected with yet. Your focus on your goal is magnetic. The Universe will rush to support your growth and your goals. So, don't give yourself so much time that you completely dilute your energy. Keep focused and know that any task will expand to fill the time allotted. Bob always says, "Just watch how fast you get the living room cleaned up between the time you hear the car door slam and the doorbell ring."

You must choose a time for the first goal's *completion*.

When would you like to see that vision manifest? Write it down.

The purpose of a date is so that we can pace our activity and set our priorities. On the other hand, when we have a project that we never set a completion date for, not surprisingly, it never is completed.

Setting a date is only a projection or a best guess, nothing more. When we tie ourselves to the date as a meter of our success, we set ourselves up for failure. If the date is met within that timeframe, we're successful. If it's not, we're unsuccessful. This is a dangerous game, given that many of the elements for achievement are not under our control.

Set your date and do your best to move the project forward daily. If unexpected changes or opportunities occur, adjust. Life must be lived each moment as it arrives and we do our best to move our projects forward. Completion dates are always under our control and are simply internal motivators to keep the energy moving. The Quakers have a saying, "Pray and move your feet." They know the fields will only flourish in the fall if they till, plant and cultivate in the spring.

Your goal needs to be *specific* and *measurable*.

Terms like "lotsa and enough" aren't specific enough to work toward. How do you know when you get to lotsa? In building our first Hogan we needed to know where the center would be, how long the walls would be, we knew they needed to be nine logs high with the door to the east, no windows and a smoke hole in the center of the ceiling. Although we have a spiritual vision of this project and the medicine man can already feel the energy speaking to him from the earth, the specifics are essential. Everyone associated with this project knows that.

Make the goal *big*...big enough that you have to *grow* in your *relationship* with yourself, others and God.

The purpose of a goal is to cause you to grow. If you already know how you will achieve a certain goal...it's not big enough. Choose something that scares and excites you at the same time. Get some juice going for growing, adventure and life. Kick it up a notch!

Include a statement of what *quality* service you will *give* in return for the result.

Goals are always a result of service rendered. What service will you render to the people who will be your clients, customers or beneficiaries? This short statement can begin, "In return for (your goal) I will give (what quality) service to (who)." An example from my vision statement reads, "We give people more than they expect through providing the most authentic, thoughtful and meaningful experiences possible, a comfortable and well-maintained venue, valuable seminars, life-changing coaching, and on-going support." Say what you'll give and then deliver it.

Now, *write it* down.

Bob has people begin their goal statement with "I'm so happy and grateful now that..." This is a powerful idea because it puts you in to an elevated energy each time you read it. You cannot be fearful while you're being happy and grateful.

Once you have done this you will **create** benchmarks for the **completion** of certain phases of your creation.

These benchmarks will contain dates for completion and what will be completed. Know that this plan and the associated dates may flex. This is fine. Many people work in three-month increments. Your dates need not be this linear, or they may. The idea here is for you to create a plan for your focused and intentional action.

Bob compares this process to taking a road trip from one coast to the other for a family wedding. The wedding is your final goal but each day you get to the next destination you have planned. These daily goals are your benchmark goals and in terms of what we're talking about, these can take weeks or months to accomplish.

I have benchmarks for each phase of our construction. I began with when I'd like to see the Hogan built and then have created a timeline back to the present from there. The next closest construction phase is looked at in terms of what is needed in manpower, supplies and preparation.

Look at the benchmark closest to the present time. This is your first task or goal. Look at the calendar. What must you do in order to support reaching this benchmark? What should your daily and weekly activity be in order to enlist the help of others and also for you to learn and do all that you must to grow into the person who creates this first benchmark? Create a daily plan of action for each day. Visualizing your goal and reading inspirational literature is not enough. These daily actions must be active goal achieving actions. A medicine man once told me something regarding training a horse that very much relates, "You must give the horse everything it needs to become what you envision for it." With your goal, you must give it all the support you can, each day, and then release it, knowing that the empty spaces will be filled by Spirit.

Each night before you go to sleep
create the ***intention*** for what it is
that you desire to create the next day
to support the ***manifestation*** of that ***goal***.

Ask God or Spirit for creative and practical help in doing this. Then open your mind to the inspiration you require to create what you intend.

Rise each day ready and excited to create your dream. Be expectant of the miracles that will abound in your day. Be grateful in advance and think only thoughts that support the arrival of those miracles. This is the dynamic process of intentional manifestation.

The Navajos rise before dawn and run to the east to greet the rising sun. As the sun breaks over the horizon they set the intention of what they desire to create that day. They then ask Spirit to support them in that plan.

How ever you choose to do this, signal your subconscious mind that you have opened the space for help.

Living intentionally means setting a pace for the creation of your vision and then living in faith that all you *must do* is all that you *can do* to support its manifestation. This takes judgment completely out of the picture. After all, judgment is a lower energy thought and will weaken the inspired process. Please remember that if you find yourself occasionally slipping into old patterns of limiting thinking, simply guide yourself gently back to more inspired thoughts. The more you do this, the more these new thoughts will become the norm. When in-tune we open a clear path from ourselves toward our desired result and then steadily attract our desired good into our lives.

I have had many clients ask **how** to tap in to attraction.

We're not used to attracting the good we desire. We're good at going out and getting the good that we desire. Let's look at attraction.

Raymond Holliwell, in his book *Working With the Law* states that there are three steps to attraction: Interest > Attention > Expectation. These steps will help you better understand how attraction relates to you.

Interest is a far bigger concept than the term casually implies. Many people unconsciously focus their interest on the things they don't want in their lives. Although they want health, wealth and happiness, they focus their interest on illness, poverty and discontent. They want wealth but look at their checkbook balance and bills as if they were determiners of their future financial success. So rather than focusing on abundance, they focus instead on lack and consequently attract more lack in their lives. It's through disciplined thinking that we focus only on the thoughts that are supportive, prosperous, joyful, and healthy.

Regarding *attention*, Holliwell states that having a high interest level is not enough. We must also be actively using attention. Think of the difference between these two concepts in terms of romantic relationships. If you are to have interest alone in a certain individual, they may never know that you care for them. It is when you focus attention on them and actively express your interest through acts of love that you really get their attention.

As we focus our attention on our purpose, we create a stream of creative energy. Thinking a stream of ideas that are in complete harmony with your project results in pure magnetism. Thinking about the magnetic power of this energy force is exciting. At this step in the process we begin to see the people, ideas and events that we need to create our dream being drawn to us. A word of warning, we must not try to organize and control these events. Doing this will pull the process back to our finite ego instead of releasing it to Universal Intelligence. We need to let go of our ego while we _support_ and _allow_ the flow. Trying to script God is useless and will only focus our attention on what we can create alone. The phrase, "Let go and let God." Summarizes this idea.

Lastly, he says to fully *expect* our intended result. This means having complete faith that the good that we desire is already ours and in fact is our birthright. Belief and expectation are the great accelerators to this process. Using the relationship example again, when we believe that a person we have an interest in feels the same, we accelerate our thoughts and actions. We think about that person constantly and come up with countless ways to show them that we care. We would never undertake this action if we didn't have faith that it would happen.

In addition to working with the natural laws, there are ten personal **mind-sets** that without fail **support** the creation of your **dreams**.

I've worked with people from across the globe to set and reach goals. Here is an overview of the best practices to support your intentional success.

First and foremost is the **belief** that we are a **part of** a far greater **whole**.

We are individualized sparks of the Creator and as such our nature is inherently creative. When we understand this, the intentions we set are about creating greatness, service, richness and love in our own lives and the lives of others. We let go of personal gratification and ego as the determiner of our success because that only serves to separate us. Instead, we embrace the interconnectedness of each to the other and to the whole. This is far greater than an intellectual understanding. It is about surrendering to the nature of God and letting go of ego.

Stephen Covey states in his poignant book
The Seven Habits of Highly Effective People
we must begin with the end in mind.

Beginning with our purpose is truly beginning with the end in mind. This process encourages us to identify and then honor the gifts we bring to this world. Your time working on your purpose has been well spent.

In addition, as you move forward on creating your vision of a purposeful life, take time to see your end result in full splendor. Picture its many details. See yourself enjoying the result in different ways. I imagine the blessing ceremony we will have as our new center opens with wonderful, supportive people attending. I can see myself sitting on a pillow leaning on the inside wall of the Hogan, enjoying the stories of a Navajo elder, with a group of like-minded global travelers. I also image signing my book for hundreds of people and hearing the wonderful stories of their own purpose discovery. Imagine all different aspects of your success to keep your brilliant mind engaged with the vision.

As Howard sat on the earth and watched his brother level the ground for the Hogan, he said he could see the whole project completed. He felt the earth was pleased. Imaging is a very spiritual process.

As you **create** your **vision** of a new life,
you will **challenge** past images and self-defeating habits.

When you enter brand new territory it will be natural to doubt. Let go. When you see doubt raise its head in the sea of your thoughts, shift your focus. Our natural desire is to fear these thoughts or feel guilt for their appearance. Maintain an objective view of them and remind yourself that guilt and fear are mere remnants of old thinking patterns that no longer serve you. Release them lovingly.

Our emotional attachment **determines**
our future results.

If we're focused on the past result, we'll simply get more of that. If we're focused and emotionally connected to our purpose, vision and intention, that is where we will go. Our emotionality is incredibly magnetic and also creates directionality. If our minds say that we want a new home but every time we think of that home we immediately feel there is no way we can afford it, our emotions or hearts will dictate the result. Our hearts are our direct line to Infinite Intelligence. Listen to your heart. What are you sending as requests to God? As Mike Dooley says, "Thoughts are things. Think good ones."

Replace **thoughts** of doubt and lack with thoughts that **align** with your **purpose**.

Our minds cannot simultaneously focus on two opposing feelings at once. When we focus on belief, doubt cannot be entertained. Effectively using our will to gently release thoughts that don't align with our highest nature and replace them with thoughts that do, is brilliance in action. This is where affirmations are very powerful.

Act as the person you have pictured yourself becoming.

Think forward and imagine what kind of man or woman you will be once you have created the purposeful projects that you have imaged. Define this person. How do they think? What do they do? How do they respond to people who cannot benefit them? How do they respond in difficult situations? What do they do daily to support the manifestation of their projects? Act as this person every moment of every day. While attending to your obligations, put some energy behind moving your projects forward every day.

I have learned to enter any new situation with calm confidence. I recently attended the New Mexico Governor's Summit on Economic Development. The women I had planned to attend the opening reception with were delayed. I could go...or not. There really was no choice for me. I was there for a purpose. It wasn't about me at all. It was about the service that the project would give. I paused at the door, took a breath and entered the room. I saw myself as the woman who was creating an amazing and exciting project that everyone wanted to hear about. I made myself put my hand out and introduce myself to every person I came face to face with. People listened to my quick overview of the project and began to network on my behalf, introducing me to those who they knew I needed to meet. I left that conference having made incredibly important alliances with people who have pledged their support. It would have never happened if I had not acted as the person I had imaged leading this project.

This simple process is very potent. It acts to close the gap, with lightening speed, between where you are and where you are going. When you can see evidence of your intention manifesting around you and begin to see yourself as the person who has already achieved your goal you have created a vibrational harmony between you and your intention. It's like two magnets whose magnetic energy are perfectly matched. They can't resist each other.

Associate with people who **believe** in you
and **see** only your **greatest good**.

Napoleon Hill says, "Deliberately seek the company of people who influence you to think and act on building the life you desire." Share inspirational thoughts and books with them. Support them. Mastermind groups that support each member to create the life they envision are very powerful. If you do form a mastermind group, join for what you can contribute, not what you can get.

Living by *intention*
calls us to always follow divine *inspiration*.

If you get a hunch to speak to someone, do. If you are led to attend a specific event, go. If a certain book calls to you, read it. Know that as you answer the call of inspiration, the volume of future signals will increase in number and clarity. This is the best way to increase your intuition. Your faith and resulting actions increase your ability to recognize the presence of inspiration in your life. The voice of the Infinite is whispering to you. Listen.

Release your attachment to outcomes.

When we try to determine how a goal or intention will manifest itself, we are attempting to script the Infinite. Divine Intelligence, or God, needs no scripting. In fact, controlling the manifestation process in this way is like jumping back into the drivers seat and pushing God out of the way. It's difficult for people to release that control. We are used to controlling every aspect of our lives and relationships. To conceive of something that works better without being controlled takes a giant leap of faith.

Consider this. My initial vision for Oso Vista Ranch was to build Santa Fe style casitas or guest cottages. I imagined that vision frequently. One day a friend mentioned that I might consider what the land desired to be. This was an out-of-the-box idea for me but I was open. I asked how to do this and was told to simply ask. I prayerfully walked on the top of the ridge opening my heart to inspiration. As I sat on a large rock in quiet meditation, I was told to build a Hogan. I didn't understand why, I simply agreed. If I had been attached to the outcome of a Santa Fe style retreat center, I would have missed this amazing journey, which is a perfect match for my heart and soul.

Live in *gratitude*.

Gratitude resides on the inspirational end of Hawkin's Map of Human Consciousness and magnetically draws us into greater alignment with the Creator. This inspired space is where all possibility exists.

I had created the business brief for the Cultural Center project and had spent much time speaking to leaders in Santa Fe and Albuquerque. I sat in my living room and showed Howard the plan for the project and talked about how we could help move it forward. He stopped, proposal in his lap and said "You were given inspiration on the ridge. Did you ever do an offering in return?" I hadn't! Although I had gratitude in my heart for the idea and was doing all I could to support it happening, I hadn't taken the time to thank Spirit for the inspired idea.

"Go to the ridge and make a corn meal offering." Howard told me. "White corn meal before noon and yellow after noon. Just a pinch is all you need. It's a symbol of your gratitude."

I asked him what he carried his corn meal in, imagining a leather medicine bad with fringe. "A bag." He answered. "A leather bag?" I asked. "No, a plastic bag. You know, a baggie. You'll want to put the baggie in the refrigerator so the corn meal doesn't get bugs in it." He winced, "That would be gross."

I smiled at the juxtaposition of traditional with modern and loved the "realness" of it.

I did do blessings on the ridge the next day with my yellow corn meal in my baggie. I thanked the spirits in every spot I was inspired to thank them in, leaving pinches of corn meal here and there, until I heard a voice in my head say, "Stop, we get it that you're grateful." I smiled at the connection to the wisdom of the ages and the Spirit of God.

Since that day doors have opened for the Oso Vista project with constant regularity. I urge you, as Howard did me, give thanks in whatever way you feel most comfortable; pray, tithe, donate, give service, bless, sing, or dance. It closes the intentional gap between your dreams and your desired results and orients your heart and soul into partnership with your Creator. There is not a more amazing place to live the life you love.

"I came to realize that life lived to
help others is the only one that matters
and that it is my duty,
in return for the lavish life
God has devolved upon me,
to help others He has placed in my path.
This is my highest and best use
as a human."

"Faith is not believing that God can.
It is knowing that God will."

Ben *Stein*

Chapter 8

Living *Intentionally*

"Your purpose is to be revealed to you
so that you can spread your wings and
cover this earth with that which is your creation."

Tony **Burroughs**

$\mathcal{I}$ was walking by the canal near my home the other morning, as I do almost every day. I love the early mornings in the southwest. The days are fresh and cool. The lovely morning sun casts rays of light from behind the clouds. In the fall the geese take off from the small lakes nearby honking and heading for the large reservoirs in the mountains.

I especially enjoy the ducks. They remind me of my mother, who made her transition a few years back. She enjoyed saving stale bread and going to the lake to feed the ducks.

I love watching the fuzzy young ducklings in the spring, swimming behind their mother, learning the ropes. They grow so quickly, and in a short amount of time they become teenagers paddling upstream in meandering flocks, forever seeking tasty snacks.

The other morning though, I witnessed something fascinating. In my two years of walking this canal I had never seen this before. Nature was revealing her wisdom to me. Fifteen ducks were treading water, in a line across the gentle flow of the canal, spaced side by side from one bank to the other with the precision of a dance line. They all faced upstream and slowly paddled in place while the river brought a banquet to them. I stopped to watch as they expended little effort to dip their beaks into the water and feast.

The beauty of it amazed me. There was no frantic energy expended, no concern for enough, and no competition. They simply positioned themselves in the abundant flow, expecting to be fed and enjoyed the prosperity of the river. It was perfect.

As I stood in awe of the beauty and order of this I reflected on all of these principles and thought, "It truly is that simple for us as well."

When we see ourselves as individualized sparks of God, our whole world shifts. We surrender our ego and find our greatness. As powerful co-creators, we then live in alignment with highly evolved thoughts and act with clarity using our talents, gifts, passions and energy to serve humanity. We envision meaningful and abundant lives as we play-out our purpose through business projects, community service and living in reverent connection with each other and the planet.

We picture what we desire to create using our powerful imaginations and then take the first step to bring it in to form using words. We live in gratitude for the abundant flow that we are a part of, always keeping our thoughts and actions in complete harmony with the pure love of the creator. We expect abundance as we live intentionally and go to work to support the physical manifestation of our desires.

We love the adventure of self-discovery and growing awareness. We connect deeply and creatively to those around us, encouraging them at every opportunity. We love each moment as we watch the beautiful miracle of creation unfold.

We make certain to maintain the thoughts that the Navajos call, "The Beauty Way"... cooperation, abundance, acceptance, gratitude, joy, support, faith, and kindness. We know that the Infinite's pure creative, loving energy is our guide. With this orientation, the world is a beautiful, wondrous place in which to learn, to live, and to love.

I'm grateful that our lives have connected. I encourage you to go out and as Gandhi says, "Be the change you want to see in the world." Your purpose calls you to your magnificence...answer.

About Margaret Merrill

Margaret Merrill has been dedicated to changing lives for over 25 years. Growing up in New York State, the forth of six children, Margaret was always a bit different. She loved the ethnic communities that thrived within her hometown and craved a deeper understanding of different cultures.

This thirst for knowledge, that she intrinsically knew came from travel, drew her to Italy to study the Renaissance and then out to the Ramah Navajo Reservation in New Mexico to complete her student teaching requirement as an art teacher.

She fell in love with the children that openly taught her about the practical and ceremonial uses of the plants that grew in the high-desert mountains and accepted a teaching position at this fascinating self-determined school. It was at this school that she stayed and taught for over twenty years.

In a desire to help her native students develop a more self-empowered mind set, she devoured self-help books, listened intently to hundreds of motivational tapes and attended countless personal development seminars. She approached this study with passion, looking for the answers that would bring more meaning and success to the lives of her first students. The results of this study changed not only the lives of her students but unexpectedly changed her life as well.

She realized that she loved teaching personal development principles and found great joy in seeing the lives of others change dramatically as a result. She took her talent for communicating complex principles, mixed it with her passion for helping others live to their greater potential and added a new venue for her teaching by creating many powerful personal development weekend seminars that touched thousands of business and professional people all over North America.

Bob Proctor, chairman of Life Success Productions, a global human resource organization, saw in Margaret a special talent for communicating what can sometimes be very complicated concepts, in a very understandable manner. He asked Margaret to facilitate his company's life success programs. She accepted and very quickly became one of his top facilitators worldwide. At which point Proctor invited her to join his staff. Through this work, she has had the opportunity to support hundreds of clients from all over the world.

Margaret realized that many of these people had one great need that kept them from experiencing their full potential, one after another had no idea what their purpose was or how to live it intentionally. As with her native students, she saw a need and determined to fill it.

She began researching the best practices for purpose discovery and as a result developed a unique method of helping individuals from all walks of life to recognize and establish their purpose, why they are here. This practice proved to be very effective for Bob's clients in eliminating confusion and frustration by creating meaningful focus in thoughts and thus results.

Margaret decided to bring this process, couched in stories and examples from her life with the Ramah Navajo, into print. "Live The Life You Love" effectively leads her readers, clients and audiences through the process of infusing their lives with purposeful living: creating profitable businesses, projects, and products that give meaningful service to humanity.

Drawn back to her love for culture, spiritual development and personal growth and compelled by a vision given to her near an ancient Anasazi ruin, she is again collaborating with the Ramah Navajo people. In partnership with her long time medicine man friend and tribal leaders, she is creating her pristine 88-acre ranch in New Mexico as a cultural and spiritual destination that will create a bridge between the Ramah Navajos and the global community.

This project is enthusiastically supported by her senator, state representatives, New Mexico cabinet secretaries and esteemed tribal leaders.

Oso Vista Ranch provides an environment for the people of the world to authentically experience the richness and healing of Navajo culture and spiritualism directly from the Navajo medicine men, storytellers, elders and artisans, gain empowered personal awareness and increased global understanding.

In her desire to serve the community that has been her home for over 25 years, Margaret also offers Oso Vista's cultural center to the Ramah Navajo Community so that they may receive traditional Navajo behavioral health services.

Margaret encourages you to courageously open your arms to those things you hold most valuable and allow her work to give you the proven framework to live them intentionally.

Margaret is currently accepting a limited number of clients for both purpose discovery and life coaching. Contact her at **margaret@fulfillyourpurpose.com** or **888.214.7493** for a free consultation.

A breathtaking purpose discovery weekend experience is also an option to you. Margaret works with small groups at her pristine New Mexico mountain ranch. To visit her ranch and take a photo tour visit **http://osovistaranch.com**.

For information regarding these productive, spiritual and intimate weekend experiences email info@fulfillyourpurpose.com.

Live The Life You Love
Margaret *Merrill*
(c) 2006 New Vision Seminars, Inc.
http://www.fulfillyourpurpose.com

Congratulations

You've finished the book!
Here's What You *Discovered*...

Through the powerful Purpose Discovery Expansion and Expression Process you've defined your values, discovered your talents, created a purpose and statement and projected that purpose into your life through a well-written vision statement.

As a result, you hold in your hands the tools to create the life of meaning you've always dreamed of. This is fantastic progress! Now that you have the blueprint and the tools, it's time to take action!

Two Important Questions
You Must *Consider* This Very Moment...

☼ Where do you go from here?

☼ How will you use this valuable work you've done to create the life you've searched for?

I'm Here To *Help* You *Take Action*!

Over the past few years I have helped hundreds of clients worldwide work through THEIR answers to these very personal questions, so I know how daunting these next crucial steps can feel. In the process, I've learned which practices are the very best! Better yet, I have produced a simple four-step system to support you in transforming your newly minted purpose statement into active and successful Purpose Centered Projects.

My simple step-by-step Purpose Centered Framework gives you everything you need to create foundations, businesses, grants and service projects! And when you've created your own Purpose Centered Projects, you instantly become a part of an up-and-coming group of compassionate, purpose-centered business people who are changing the world by living lives they love! Like Bill and Melinda Gates, Warren Buffett, Ted Turner or Oprah - you're now in league with like-minded others who want to improve the world! How cool is that?

Your Next Step...Here's What You *Need To Do* Right Now

Sign Up For My Platinum Purpose Centered Projects Teleseminar And Receive My Expert Help.

Here Is The Four-Step Process That Will Support You In Creating Your Purpose Centered Project....

❂ Purpose Based Think Tank We'll use guided imagery and brainstorming processes to create a list of possible Purpose Centered Projects.

✪ Purpose Centered Visioning-This expansion process supports your effort to begin with the end in mind. You'll choose one idea from your Project Think-Tank list and I'll guide you through the process of creating a focused, action-oriented vision statement that will move you inspirationally toward your desired end result. Imagination is key to the power of this process.

✪ Purpose Based Goal Achieving-Here you'll develop a specific and measurable goal statement based on giving quality service to the beneficiaries you've identified in your Purpose Statement. Prosperity is the natural outgrowth of this service-centered process.

✪ Purpose Centered Project Planning-Finally, we'll apply a project timeline to your visions, creating focused benchmark goals and purposeful daily action to assure your success.

This Program Is Unique: If You're Seeking a Comprehensive Purpose Discovery and Development System To Guide Your Project Development Efforts, This is IT!

There's simply not another one out there. I know, because I looked for one myself, before I created this one - and I've had financial planners tell me they've unsuccessfully conducted similar searches. (And they now send their clients to me.)

This Material Is Worth **Millions** To You!

Once you complete the Platinum Process you will confidently hold the keys to your new life—a life that you love every minute of every day. And you'll know how to use them! You will know how to create the prosperity you desire—because when you're living your purpose, inspiration follows you, attracting to you every support you need to live the life you've always dreamed of.

So **Here** Is The Bottom Line:

Twenty years from now, you will find yourself doing one of two things: either looking back at a life well-lived OR wondering how your life might have been more satisfactory, had you taken the opportunity you have in your hands right now.

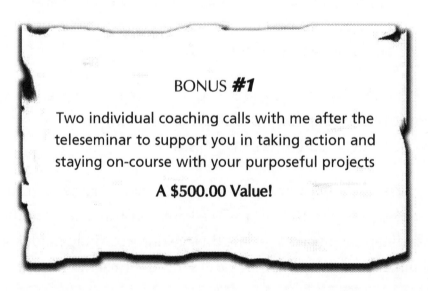

BONUS **#1**

Two individual coaching calls with me after the teleseminar to support you in taking action and staying on-course with your purposeful projects

A $500.00 Value!

BONUS **#2**

$1500.00 off my Purpose Quest Retreat!

Imagine yourself in an intimate group, at my pristine New Mexico mountain ranch, setting up the plan to carry your purpose far beyond your life. See yourself masterminding your project with leaders from around the world, creating valuable alliances and connecting with the resources you need. Be a part of the purposeful revolution that is sweeping the world!

Yes, $1500 off!
Why? Because I'm committed to helping you
"Live The Life You Love".

BONUS **#3**

Access to my network of grants and contracts, publishing, marketing, investment, business consulting and foundations professionals

A $1000 Value!

<u>Don't **Live** By Regrets.</u>

Don't Miss This Exciting Offer **Valued At Over $4000** But Priced To **Include You**!

Act now to change the course of your life and become part of the purposeful revolution that is sweeping the world!

Go to www.fulfillyourpurpose.com and **SIGN UP NOW** for more information on these Powerful Programs!

Printed in the USA
CPSIA information can be obtained
at www.ICGtesting.com
JSHW082212140824
68134JS00014B/579

9 781600 370014